# Secure

# Secure

THE REVOLUTIONARY
GUIDE *to* CREATING
*a* SECURE LIFE

Amir Levine

**Cornerstone Press**

Cornerstone Press

UK | USA | Canada | Ireland | Australia
India | New Zealand | South Africa

Cornerstone Press is part of the Penguin Random House group of companies
whose addresses can be found at global.penguinrandomhouse.com

Penguin Random House UK,
One Embassy Gardens, 8 Viaduct Gardens, London SW11 7BW

penguin.co.uk

First published in the US by Tarcher, an imprint of
Penguin Random House LLC, New York 2026
First published in the UK by Cornerstone Press 2026
001

Copyright © Secure LLC, 2026

The moral right of the author has been asserted

Penguin Random House values and supports copyright. Copyright fuels creativity, encourages diverse voices, promotes freedom of expression and supports a vibrant culture. Thank you for purchasing an authorised edition of this book and for respecting intellectual property laws by not reproducing, scanning or distributing any part of it by any means without permission. You are supporting authors and enabling Penguin Random House to continue to publish books for everyone. No part of this book may be used or reproduced in any manner for the purpose of training artificial intelligence technologies or systems. In accordance with Article 4(3) of the DSM Directive 2019/790, Penguin Random House expressly reserves this work from the text and data mining exception.

Book design by Meighan Cavanaugh

The flowchart on page 35 includes an AI-generated image derived from
a photo by SvetaZi, licensed from Shutterstock (Enhanced Licence).

The flowchart on page 109 includes an AI-generated image created with Adobe Firefly.

Printed and bound in Great Britain by Clays Ltd, Elcograf S.p.A.

The authorised representative in the EEA is Penguin Random House Ireland,
Morrison Chambers, 32 Nassau Street, Dublin D02 YH68

A CIP catalogue record for this book is available from the British Library

ISBN: 978-1-529-97616-8 (hardback)
ISBN: 978-1-529-97617-5 (trade paperback)

Penguin Random House is committed to a sustainable future
for our business, our readers and our planet. This book is made
from Forest Stewardship Council® certified paper.

*To my sister*

# Contents

*Preface*
Touched by Secure Magic..................................................................... *xi*

*Introduction*
Changing the Brain for Greater Security: From Psychoanalysis
to Neuroscience and Back....................................................................... *1*

## PART I
## The Secure Brain

1. The Cyberball Effect ........................................................................ 15

2. A Life of CARRP: Fostering Hyperconnectedness...................... 25

3. Neuroplasticity: The Science (and Art) of SIMIs ....................... 37

## PART II
## Living in Secure Mode

4. Harnessing Your Brain's Energy to Maximize Your Potential....55

5. Discover Your Attachment Style—in All Areas of Your Life ..... 71

6. The Anxious Attachment Style: Living with Perceptual Superpowers ........................................................... *95*

7. The Avoidant Attachment Style: Living Comfortably with a Measure of Distance ............................................... *123*

8. The Fearful Avoidant: Taking a Leap of Faith into Closeness ...... *143*

9. Test-Drive Your Attachment Knowledge ........................ *155*

## PART III

# The Secure Mind

10. Causality: Recasting Your Past from a Secure Stance ............ *171*

11. The Comparing and Collaborative Brain: Finding the Right People to Count On ............................................. *183*

12. Secure Priming Therapy: Unearthing Hidden Sparks of Talent ................................................... *203*

13. Secure Coaching: Learning to Be Secure in Real Time .......... *221*

*Afterword*
Your Secure Practice .............................................. *249*
*Acknowledgments* ................................................. *251*
*Index* ............................................................ *253*

# Author's Note

When I first encountered the science of adult attachment styles more than a decade ago, I experienced it as a revelation. It was like seeing our relational world in color after only observing shades of gray. The four styles—anxious (craving closeness but fearing rejection), avoidant (preferring independence over closeness), fearful avoidant (a mix of the two), and secure (comfortable with closeness and easygoing)—gave me a new language to understand how people connect. That insight eventually led to my first book, *Attached*.

Since then, attachment science—as well as my own growth and understanding of what it means to be secure—has expanded by leaps and bounds.

In these pages, I present for the first time a new set of tools that I developed to help you become more secure not only in romantic relationships but in all areas of life—with friends, family, colleagues, and even with yourself.

This framework is grounded in decades of neuroscience and attachment research and would not have been possible without the contributions of

## AUTHOR'S NOTE

researchers in this field from across the globe. I am enormously grateful to the brilliant minds whose groundbreaking work has illuminated many new facets of our behavior and how the brain works. Their contributions form the foundation on which this book stands.

For the book's notes and references, please visit amirlevinemd.com.

---

*The examples and case studies in this book are composite stories drawn from common patterns and experiences. Any resemblance to specific individuals is coincidental.*

PREFACE

# Touched by Secure Magic

When I was twelve years old, I accompanied my older sister, who was fourteen, on a weeklong beach vacation with her friend Lila and Lila's mom, Ruth. We stayed in an old, somewhat dilapidated beach house perched on the edge of a cliff overlooking the ocean. It was August, and every day we would race down a short, winding trail to the beach, ride the waves, and soak up the sun. Then we'd climb back up the hill, hose ourselves down in the garden to rinse off the salt water, pat ourselves dry, and run into the house to get ice cream. We ate hearty meals, played board games, and occasionally went into town to explore.

I was grateful to my sister for inviting me to join her, and to Ruth for agreeing to include me in her family's vacation. It was no small feat to host two more teenagers, one of whom she had never met, on a weeklong summer getaway. Ruth, like her biblical counterpart, was an incredibly gracious host. We immediately felt at home. She exuded calmness and tranquility, wore a patient smile, and spoke in a way that showed she cared deeply and that we mattered. If there was even a hint of tension between

## PREFACE

us kids, she had a knack for defusing it effortlessly. She never really told us what to do or when to do it, but somehow we knew, and we wanted to do the right thing when we were around her.

I wasn't the only one touched by Ruth's essence. She was a third-grade teacher, and many of her students kept in touch with her decades after they graduated. She seemed to effortlessly serve as a nurturing presence in the lives of everyone around her. It's not that her life was without challenges. After her husband died at forty-six from heart disease, she was left to care for two daughters on her own and had to change her vocation to support them. She became a TV producer at a prominent network, which at the time was primarily a man's world, and she produced a collection of award-winning documentaries.

I have since visited many beautiful places around the world and had other wonderful vacations, but this magical summer holiday with Ruth looms large in my memory. It was only decades later, when I stumbled across research about secure attachment, that I came to realize why that vacation stands out so strongly in my mind. It was because of Ruth.

Knowing what I know today, I realize that Ruth, who is no longer with us, was secure. "Secures" have a knack for elevating everyone around them. If you think back on your past, you can most likely spot some of your own secure experiences. And digging deeper, I suspect you will see that they were also some of the happiest moments in your life.

My sister, the reason why I was on that particular holiday in the first place, possesses the same biological talent as Ruth and has been a secure presence in my life for as long as I can remember. Since I was a small child, she's always allowed me to tag along with her wherever she went. I have never been excluded from any of her comings and goings. Some of my earliest memories are of joining her when I was four or five years old to visit her friend, because they had three cute dachshund puppies that I wanted to play with, and of tagging along with a group of her girlfriends when they went to the park.

Indeed, a whole body of research from the past few decades reveals how essential even the most minuscule secure interactions are to our happiness and well-being. The research goes a step further—it supposes that these secure interactions that occur throughout our lifetime may leave a kernel of security within us, something we can cultivate and use to become more secure ourselves.

In this book, I combine insights from secure experiences in my own life with those of my patients, students, and interviewees, along with research findings about secure attachment and the brain, to help you become more secure in an enduring way. I also draw on a method developed in my work with patients called *Secure Priming Therapy*, or *Secure Therapy* for short,* which encourages the sharing of secure memories as we seek to unearth those kernels of security within us and then use these experiences as stepping stones to become more secure in our everyday lives.

Over the years, my patients have recounted dozens of secure experiences in treatment. Some had exceptional parents; others had grandparents who were wholly devoted to them. Many described incredibly nurturing teachers and professors, spouses, mentors, bosses, and siblings who bestowed their secure talents upon them. As time has passed, my admiration for the secures of this world has grown tremendously. As I continue to listen with awe to testimonies of secure attachment, I've come to fall in love with the secures all around us. They are the ones who always show up for us—they rarely fail us or fight with us. I've realized that this talent often goes unappreciated, perhaps even ignored, possibly because secures are so solid. There's very little drama around them, leading their many gifts to go unnoticed. In contrast, in Secure Therapy, the secures in this world take center stage as they model safety and ease in their relationships with us, teaching us how to live more securely. This approach not only guides us in

---

*Secure Priming Therapy, or Secure Therapy for short, expands on social psychology research to demonstrate how secure priming methods help individuals become more secure. It also incorporates broader scientific findings, especially those related to the brain, to enhance security priming.

developing secure relationships but also sparks changes in our brains that help us recover from past adversity.

This book, like the work I do with my patients, will help you tap into these secure kernels both in you and in your world, and expand and build upon them so that you, too, can become more secure, like Ruth, my sister, and others. Living life this way, in what I have come to call *secure mode*, means that you move through the world—loving, working, befriending, and taking care of both yourself and others—in a more secure fashion.

## THE FAR-REACHING EFFECTS OF LIVING IN SECURE MODE

Recent scientific discoveries have revealed that living life in secure mode has the power to positively impact many different facets of our lives. The studies show that the advantage of living securely extends far and wide, well beyond the scope of just romantic relationships, affecting how you view yourself, the world around you, and your relationships in general. For example, studies find that if you're secure, you tend to navigate social media better, avoiding the negative impacts that insecure individuals often experience—like obsessing over how they may be perceived by others or interpreting a lack of likes as rejection. When it comes to shopping, you're less swayed by consumerism; logos and brands hold much less appeal. In terms of health and disease, you tend to be healthier over time and have a better relationship with your health-care providers. When you do have a difficult illness, whether cancer or a chronic, painful condition such as fibromyalgia, you have fewer physical symptoms and you handle the ailment better emotionally—you get less depressed, and your overall outlook on life is less affected by your illness. Even when you're looking for a job, if you're secure, you tend to be much more upbeat about it. You're

PREFACE

more effective in your search and the process doesn't negatively impact you as much—it doesn't take away from your self-esteem.

So, to summarize dozens of studies, life is much less emotionally taxing when you're secure! Living securely, it seems, frees you up to devote time to things that really matter, giving you the opportunity to befriend, parent, create, and explore.

But how can you become more consistently secure?

Brain imaging studies show time and again that people who are securely attached differ from those who are insecurely attached in both the way their brain is structured and how it functions. Certain areas of the brain that are related to anxiety and stress are especially affected. To become more secure, you literally have to find a way to change the structure and workings of your brain. But how does one go about doing that? The answer came to me in a most fortuitous way.

Secure

INTRODUCTION

# Changing the Brain for Greater Security: From Psychoanalysis to Neuroscience and Back

How can you change your brain to become more secure and improve your life? By changing the physical structure of it. But how does one achieve that? You'd think this was something I learned in my training to become a psychiatrist, but that wasn't entirely the case. Instead, I stumbled upon the answer in the way things often happen—by chance.

Since early in my adult life, I wanted to become a psychoanalyst. The idea of helping people find more satisfaction in their lives by changing unhelpful patterns through talk therapy was very appealing to me. I even went into a yearlong analysis, lying on the infamous couch four times a week, a prerequisite for analytic school. I immersed myself in the writings of Freud and his followers, and my supervisors in residency all expected me to go on to analytic training. I had my future mapped out. Never in a thousand years did I think I would end up at a lab bench, pipetting samples of DNA, RNA, and protein into small tubes to examine the molecular underpinnings of how the brain changes. But that's exactly what happened.

In many ways, I owe my career choice to my own analysis. During that year of preparing for analytic school, I had to choose a subject for research at the university. In my free associations on the couch, I rediscovered my love and aptitude for basic biology and chemistry, and because of that, I found the courage to pursue a career for which I had little skill. At the time, I couldn't tell one piece of lab equipment from another, let alone run elaborate molecular experiments from start to finish.

One of my mentors in residency, Professor Abby Fyer, gave me some advice about deciding on a research topic. "A researcher's life is a hard life," she said. "You will be the recipient of a lot of rejection and criticism and will experience many setbacks. To survive, you need to choose something that you really have a passion for, something that provides you with the motivation to put in the sustained, often unrewarded effort that is an integral part of our profession." Heeding her warning, I set off to find a topic that I was passionate about. I read dozens of research papers published by people in my department on topics that interested me. One paper in the journal *Cell* stood out—it was about how lasting memories are formed at the molecular level.

I asked to meet with the senior author on that paper, Eric Kandel, a Nobel laureate. Nervously, I began telling him about my interest in his work, especially in the *Cell* publication, but also about my lack of experience. After two minutes, he got up and asked me to follow him. He took me up a flight of stairs to introduce me to the person who masterminded the project, James Schwartz, whom everyone called Jimmy.

## EPIGENETICS, THE ENVIRONMENT, AND YOUR BRAIN

Jimmy's paper was about how adding certain molecular tags (or *switches*) to DNA in the brain is a prerequisite for the formation of long-term memory. Jimmy and his postdoc, Zhonghui Guan, in collaboration with Eric Kandel's lab, showed that if you excite the huge neurons in the sea slug

## CHANGING THE BRAIN FOR GREATER SECURITY

*Aplysia*, molecular tags are added on top of the DNA in those cells. The addition of the DNA tags boosts gene expression, which in turn leads to long-term memory and learning. The researchers went on to suggest that the same process occurs in humans when learning takes place. This means that if you remember any of this introduction tomorrow, specific molecular tags must have been added to the DNA in your brain. In essence, they demonstrated that this process, a form of epigenetic change,* is crucial for memory formation. Think of these tags as tiny bookmarks or switches that help your brain know which pages to reread and which circuits to turn on so a new memory can stick.

I didn't know it at the time, but this paper and one that followed from Eric Kandel's lab were seminal works that, along with other papers from that period, launched the field of epigenetics in neuroscience. After these two papers came out, the entire field exploded: Findings about epigenetics in addiction, memory and learning, maternal behavior, and other areas in neuroscience were reported by dozens of groups around the globe. Over the next decade it became apparent that epigenetic changes in the central nervous system are the primary mechanism that keeps the brain plastic—an important way in which life events can structurally mold our brains and help us change who we are across our lifespans, even in old age. The catch is to find environments that will facilitate favorable changes in our brains.

Of course, back when I first read the *Aplysia* paper in *Cell*, I had no way of knowing what the future would hold. In that specific moment, I simply found the work interesting and creative, and I thought it was what I'd like to focus on. I discussed the paper with Jimmy, enthusiastically suggesting some ideas and critiques of my own, and at the end of the con-

---

*Epigenetic changes are ones that occur "on top of" the DNA, like the molecular tags mentioned earlier. These tags change the expression of our genes—and ultimately us—without altering our genetic code.

versation he offered me work in his lab for three months—a trial run to see how I would fare.

So there I was—in a lab, at the bench, learning how to conduct molecular biology experiments. Jimmy and I also began to meet regularly to discuss science, literature, and other interesting topics. We brainstormed about potential research projects. Three months flew by. Jimmy was an incredible mentor and an original thinker. He took a chance on me when most investigators would have politely refused to employ such a rookie in their lab. The work was far from easy. I remember the first time I really messed up: I was doing a labor-intensive and expensive three-day experiment isolating a special formulation of DNA, along with its tags, from brain tissue. At the end of the third day, I threw out the supernatant—the liquid that was lying on top—and proudly showed the technician the beautiful pellet that was sitting at the bottom of the tube, only to find out that the supernatant was where my desired DNA was, and the pellet was just cellular debris to be disposed of. I was mortified, thinking Jimmy would throw me out of the lab, but instead he told me, "Don't worry, you'll get the hang of it. You made an error; it's not the end of the world." He then added, "Being a good scientist is not only about practical knowledge. Being a good scientist has a lot to do with what's in there." He gestured toward my head. "It's about being creative, daring, and inquisitive." And so it is.

I stayed past the three months, and with time, I became better at the technical work. I now know that it was because of the secure environment that Jimmy created in the lab that I was able to learn a new field from scratch. Indeed, thanks to his unwavering support, I did quite well, and within a relatively short period of time, I published my first paper.

In parallel to my work as a scientist who studies the brain on a molecular level, I maintained my interest in clinical work and helping people, and my passion as a therapist found an additional outlet in writing. While doing a rotation in the therapeutic nursery in my child and adolescent psychiatry fellowship at Columbia, I serendipitously came across research emerging from the field of social psychology. This research concerned the fact that we all possess *attachment styles*—anxious, avoidant, and secure—that hugely impact the way we behave in adult relationships. Anxious people seek closeness but are very sensitive to rejection, afraid of being unloved. Avoidant people find it difficult to be close, so they emphasize self-reliance and tend to push people away. Secure people are warm and loving; they want to be close and are not afraid of being rejected.

This information came to me at just the right moment in my personal life, as I was going through a breakup. I experienced attachment research as immensely helpful, a true eye-opener, which led to an epiphany: If knowing this information was so helpful to me, it would undoubtedly be helpful to others. The only problem was that in its academic form, this information wasn't accessible or readily useful to people's everyday lives. The research data about attachment styles, buried in academic lingo, was a diamond in the rough. It needed to be excavated and transformed into a clinical tool that people could use to navigate relationships better. Over a period of close to five years, my coauthor, Rachel Heller, and I translated the information and wrote *Attached*. It was the first time that I created a clinical tool based on scientific findings. *Attached* helped a lot of people see how an understanding of attachment styles in day-to-day life can improve their ability to manage romantic relationships. But in sessions with patients, emails from readers, and interviews, the question that always arose was "How do I become more secure?"

I didn't have a complete answer to that.

The answer came in the way that I least expected. Without fully realizing it, in treatment with patients, I found myself tapping into my knowledge from the lab to better illuminate things they were experiencing. I noticed I was veering off from the usual therapeutic techniques to explain brain function as it relates to our everyday lives. Over time, this approach took center stage.

## BECOMING SECURE WITH SCIENCE—METACOGNITIVE NEUROSCIENCE

Almost two decades after I first started to work at the lab bench, I've come full circle, back to my first passion: helping people improve their lives. I do this not only through psychoanalysis but also by harnessing my knowledge of neuroscience to help people understand how to create an environment that will nourish secure brain changes. By merging three fields of knowledge—clinical psychiatry, attachment science, and basic neuroscience—I was able to devise specific tools to help align our thoughts and beliefs with the workings of our brain. I've come to call this merged field *secure-focused neuroscience* and its clinical counterpart *Secure Therapy*. Secure-focused neuroscience uses metacognitive tools that build on our ability to think about our own thoughts—to help us reflect on what we're doing and why through a more secure, brain-based lens.

I was surprised by how much of a difference secure-focused neuroscience and Secure Therapy made in the lives of my students, my patients, and my supervisees' patients. One person who had struggled with OCD for years was finally able to find the right treatment. Another, who had nearly flunked out of medical school, turned things around, graduated, and went on to residency. Patients who had dealt with social isolation were able to build rich, gratifying social lives. It didn't happen overnight, nor was it without effort on their part, but the secure-focused neuroscience knowledge and tools were remarkably helpful in freeing them from unproductive beliefs, attitudes, and notions, allowing them a greater degree of security and sustained long-term improvement.

I decided to write about this new therapy and the tools I've devised alongside it so that people beyond my immediate corner of the world could better understand the workings of their brains and apply this knowledge to their everyday lives. These tools will help you change your thoughts, perceptions, emotions, behaviors, and, no less important, social milieu, ultimately helping you become more secure.

> **SECURE PRIMING THERAPY**
>
> Secure Priming Therapy—also referred to as Secure Therapy—is a new treatment approach that merges three fields of knowledge: clinical psychology, attachment science, and basic neuroscience. This therapeutic modality, detailed throughout the book, offers practical tools designed to align our thoughts and beliefs with how the brain actually works. Secure Therapy also draws from secure priming strategies that have been proven in studies to help people become more secure.

## HOW THIS BOOK IS STRUCTURED TO HELP YOU BECOME MORE SECURE

This book is divided into three parts. In part 1, "The Secure Brain," I share my top three must-have brain-based lessons for creating a secure life. This section of the book contains three chapters, one for each lesson. It is relevant to all of us, including the secures of the world, because it speaks to the universal workings of our brain that affect us no matter what attachment style we are. It also explains how we can influence the structure of the brain epigenetically by surrounding it with the secure environment it needs to flourish. The lesson of chapter 1 is that exclusion or feeling ignored can have a pernicious effect on your brain. I've come to call exclusion the *Cyberball effect* and feeling ignored *stillfacing*, in reference to two groundbreaking experiments that I will outline. The antidote for these social harms is prioritizing connections with others that are the opposite of exclusionary, relationships that have a secure default mode of consistency, availability, responsiveness, reliability, and predictability, which I refer to with the acronym CARRP. This important concept is the focus of the second lesson, outlined in chapter 2. Finally, in chapter 3, you will learn how to create an enriched environment for yourself that will protect your brain—and you—by ensuring that the vast majority of what I've come to call the *seemingly insignificant minor interactions* of everyday life, or SIMIs for short, are CARRP.

Part 2 is about how to get into a more secure mode if you have an insecure attachment orientation. If you have an insecure style, whether anxious, avoidant, or fearful avoidant, this part of the book will lay out the steps you need to take, using the secure brain tools you learned in part 1, to build a more secure environment for yourself. Chapter 4 will explain how the brain uses energy and why understanding that is important for attaining greater security. Then, in chapter 5, you will identify your own attachment style using a research-based questionnaire known as the gold standard for determining attachment styles across various relationships: the Relationship Structures Questionnaire. Based on your attachment style, the rest of part 2 will show you how to use the tools you learned in part 1 for your betterment, with specific insights and instructions on each insecure attachment style. However, it's also important to read about the other attachment styles and how people with these styles can use the tools to gain a better understanding of the challenges they face in their quest for greater security. This will give you insight into how to get along with them better and support them on their journey to becoming more secure.

Part 3 of the book aims to secure your mind. Here you will be asked to reexamine your past like a scientist. You will learn how your brain monitors relationships around you from a collaborative perspective as well as how to use a ruling principle in biology—molecular diversity—to find secure sparks of talent within you. This section also focuses on a new type of attachment neuroscience–based treatment, Secure Therapy and Coaching. You'll already have been introduced to many of its core ideas and tools throughout parts 1 and 2, but here you'll take it a step further, learning additional strategies to help you manage real-life situations and respond in real time—as they unfold.

My hope is that by implementing the various lessons in this book, you, too, can become more secure. I've peppered the chapters with workshops and questions so you can practice the material and make it more your own.

And now, without further ado, let's turn to part 1, "The Secure Brain."

# PART I

# The Secure Brain

We tend to think of the brain as a well-protected organ, sealed off inside a thick skull, shielded from the outside world. Unlike our skin, which is exposed to the elements—requiring sunscreen, clothing, and regular care—we don't treat our brain as something that needs daily protection.

But the truth is, the brain may be the most environmentally sensitive organ in the body. It sends out delicate tendrils—our senses—to constantly monitor our surroundings, and it's being shaped by what it encounters every second. Even reading these words is changing your brain on a molecular level.

I think of part 1 as your neuroscience care manual—a guide to protecting and nurturing your social brain the way you might care for your skin. What's the social brain's version of harm? What is its "sunscreen"? Which interactions at home, at work, and with friends will keep it healthy and resilient? Part 1 will give you the tools you need to protect your social brain and, by extension, your life. This section of the book came out of a question a student once asked me: If I had to boil neuroscience findings down to a few practical insights that could help someone improve their brain and their life, what would I say?

I thought long and hard. Over the past few decades, our understanding of brain function has expanded dramatically. There are so many fascinating discoveries—so many insights into how our "control center" works. I sifted through dozens of findings and, in the end, I landed on the ones presented in this section. I've condensed them into three key lessons. These lessons form the backbone of the book—the core concepts and tools that we will use and refer to throughout the chapters that follow.

# 1

# The Cyberball Effect

## THE FRISBEE GAME THAT CHANGED EVERYTHING

Imagine a video game where you are one of three two-dimensional figures playing catch. Suddenly, the other two figures stop passing the ball to you. They continue to play with each other while you stand there, arms outstretched, waiting for the ball to be thrown in your direction, but, alas, you're completely ignored!

Dr. Kipling ("Kip") D. Williams of Purdue University, the scientist who created this video game as part of an experiment, credits the idea to an experience he had several years earlier. Williams was in the park with his dog when a Frisbee came sailing in his direction. He happily picked it up and threw it back to the two Frisbee players. They began to include Williams in their game of catch, but soon, just as suddenly as they had begun to pass him the Frisbee, they stopped. Williams remembers that being left out of the game made him feel surprisingly bad, despite not knowing the other two players and having expected that they would eventually resume their own game. This incident led him to design the video game protocol that he called the Cyberball experiment.

The Cyberball experiment is not done in an immersive, virtual reality environment. Instead, it is a rudimentary, two-dimensional game. Nothing in it seems like real life. Yet thanks to its simplicity, this game has led to one of the most far-reaching insights into how our brain responds to exclusion. When participants take part in this experiment while undergoing a functional MRI (fMRI), areas in the brain associated with pain, distress, and self-evaluation light up when their avatar is excluded. In other words, they experience exclusion as so painful that it triggers feelings of self-doubt and diminished self-worth.

It doesn't end there. Our brains are so sensitive to exclusion that there seems to be little that can be done to soften the blow. Research studies show that this Cyberball effect is immune to potential mitigating circumstances. Many interventions that one might think would lessen the painful response to exclusion don't seem to make even the slightest dent in the Cyberball effect. For example, you would think that if someone you don't particularly care for excludes you, you wouldn't mind, right?

Two studies, one by Karen Gonsalkorale and Kip Williams from the University of California, Davis, and one by Marie-Pierre Fayant from Université de Paris and colleagues, put this assumption to the test. In their experiment, students were told that the other players tossing the ball were members of the Ku Klux Klan. You might be surprised to learn that their reaction to being left out was just as strong as if they had been playing with their best friends. Exclusion by a despised group of people is just as hurtful as exclusion by people you actually like.

What about money? Will financial compensation offered in exchange for exclusion lessen its effects? In another set of studies, participants who were excluded in a Cyberball experiment received a financial incentive—they were told that they could keep a sum of money when they were excluded, whereas participants who got the ball tossed in their direction would lose money every time they got the ball. The participants who got to keep the money displayed the same adverse reaction as those who didn't get compensated. It turns out that even money doesn't help!

The conclusion from studies conducted over the span of several decades is that the human brain has been "programmed" through evolution to experience exclusion as deeply personal and profoundly painful. And—whether we like it or not—we have very little means of controlling the immediate effect. Even when we know it's make-believe, even if the exclusion is by people we don't care for, even when we're paid money to go through it.

## STILLFACING

The Cyberball effect is not exclusive to interactions among a group of three people or more. You can also feel excluded and ignored when there are only two people in the room. I call that stillfacing, after the famous "still face" experiment designed by Dr. Ed Tronick, a professor at Harvard University and the University of Massachusetts. In the experiment, a young infant and their parent are facing each other, interacting as they normally would. The parent makes funny faces and engages the infant in cute baby babble. Then the parent is asked to turn their face away for a quick moment and when they look back at their child to cease any vocal or physical interaction with the baby, remaining completely expressionless—in other words, to *stillface* them. The response from the baby is swift. They try to get the parent's attention by pointing at something, clapping their hands, or smiling. When that doesn't work, after just a few seconds they quickly turn to more extreme measures. They throw their hands up in the air and make loud shrieks, desperate for their parent's attention. When their gestures go unheeded, they turn away, become withdrawn, and often begin to cry. Thankfully, the stillfacing doesn't last long; the parent reestablishes an emotional connection with their baby quickly and the child calms down.

I believe that the stillface experiment reveals that, from a very early age, we have a neurocircuitry that loathes being ignored or emotionally disconnected. Our brain is wired to appreciate an emotional continuity with the people around us, and when that gets disrupted or stops for whatever reason, it bothers us to no end.

Oftentimes people don't realize the immense emotional power they wield when they stillface you. When confronted, they will usually say something like "What do you want from me? I didn't say anything" or "I didn't do anything; I was just sitting here minding my own business." But in truth, from the point of view of the brain, stillfacing is an aggressive act that inflicts agony on our nervous system and stirs up uncomfortable and painful emotions that lead to disconnect and, eventually, withdrawal.

In fact, being stillfaced triggers such a powerful, instinctive reaction that we can feel its effects even without realizing it, as demonstrated by the following experiment.

### Being Stillfaced Without Knowing It

Does your brain scout out your environment for potential social disconnection even without your knowledge? Or, in other words, can stillfacing affect you even when you're not aware of it?

One study, titled "To Be Looked at as Though Air: Civil Attention Matters," by Eric Wesselmann from Purdue University and colleagues, examined this question. In it, the researchers assessed the different reactions of passersby in a busy area on a university campus after a member of the research team walked toward them and fleetingly acknowledged them by making eye contact, sometimes adding a quick smile, versus when the team member didn't make eye contact at all, instead looking at them as if they were "looking through air" (the researcher was instructed to look at a point in the air beyond the person's ear, to make sure no eye contact would be made). Immediately after each encounter, another person on the research team stopped the passerby and asked them to take part in a general survey about university life, which included questions about how connected they felt to others. The survey did not indicate that they were being evaluated after an eye-contact or non-eye-contact intervention.

The researchers hypothesized that making eye contact would make people feel more connected, whereas looking through them as if they didn't exist would make them feel disconnected. They also wanted to see if adding a smile would make a difference. The findings demonstrated a clear trend that people who, unbeknownst to them, were purposefully disregarded felt less connected than if the experimenter had made eye contact with them. Interestingly, the smile didn't matter. Many of the participants did not even recall the interaction, yet they were still influenced by the experimenters' behavior. How can stillfacing affect you even if you're not fully aware of it? It turns out that your social brain is trained to constantly assess your environment, monitoring your social interactions in the background even when you're not conscious that it's happening.

## AN EYE-OPENING WALK IN THE WILD

At first, I struggled to understand the biological logic or selection advantage of the Cyberball effect and stillfacing. Why would a rudimentary two-dimensional video game involving a lapse in acknowledgment instinctively affect the brain so strongly, with our having very little say in the matter?

I finally understood the logic behind this sensitive neurocircuitry when I was on a safari in Africa and our guide took us for a walk on the reserve. We were walking outside among the wild animals. One guide walked in front and another in the back, both carrying loaded guns. We were instructed to walk in single file and not let any space form between us at any point. When one of us stalled and let a little distance form, the guide in the back immediately called out to the person to close the gap. It was from this experience that I caught a glimpse of our ancestors' lives and began to comprehend the purpose of our exquisitely sensitive-to-exclusion neurocircuitry. This is what it was programmed for—to make sure we survived as hunted animals. To alert our senses of the potential danger of being ignored by our peers even for a split second.

No wonder this neurocircuitry doesn't care about money or if you like the person who throws the ball in your direction or not. There's no time to even consider all of that; it becomes secondary in the face of a clear and present danger and our instinctive need to survive. That's why so many horror movies use the same formula to trick our brains into feeling genuinely scared—by isolating protagonists when danger lurks. Indeed, the person left alone is often the one who gets picked off.

The opposite is also true: We find great solace in the protection of our comrades. This explains why so many action movies feature teams working together, often at great risk, to save a few individuals. Beyond our natural dislike of being ignored, our brains are strongly drawn to the idea of a tight-knit group going to any lengths to rescue others. It's a reliable formula for blockbuster movie success.

## EXCLUSION HURTS YOUR SOUL

Even before the fMRI experiments were conducted, Kip Williams used the Cyberball experiments to make remarkable discoveries about how profoundly exclusion affects us psychologically. The findings were quite shocking. In studies performed over the course of several decades, Williams and colleagues discovered that exclusion affects our innermost feelings and thoughts about ourselves. Specifically, they noted that three important areas commonly thought of as entirely self-directed and not at all related to how we interact interpersonally are in fact impacted by our social environment:

1. How much you feel that life is meaningful
2. How much you feel that you're in control of your life
3. Your self-esteem

Being excluded will make you feel a reduced sense of belonging; this is expected. But why would being dissed have any effect on your attitude that life is meaningful, your feeling of being in control of your life, or your sense of self-esteem? Don't these things have more to do with self-love?

It turns out that core emotional domains such as these that we attribute to self-love are directly shaped by how others treat us; specifically, they are negatively affected when we are excluded.

The implications of these experimental findings for daily life are far-reaching. To cultivate self-love, eliminating exclusion is crucial, because exclusion damages essential emotional areas that influence your self-identity. Exclusion profoundly impacts your deepest feelings about yourself and your life, affecting aspects of your well-being that you might assume are solely related to your personal view of yourself, independent of others. Inclusion is a scientifically proven path to self-love!

## WHERE DO YOU GO FROM HERE?

We feel the pain of exclusion throughout our entire lives. It begins when we're infants, before we even start to talk, and persists until the last of our days.

You see it in babies who get "jealous" when their parents interact with each other or other siblings. You also see it in schools, in the workplace, and at home, and it can even leave a lasting sting in nursing homes or posthumously, through the wills that people leave behind.

Exclusion exacts a dire toll in every sphere of our lives both online and in the real world. It leads to withdrawal and disconnection. More profoundly, it affects the core of our being, influencing our self-esteem, our sense of life's meaning, and our perception of control over our lives.

As things stand now, I'm sure that even though you don't like the feeling of being excluded, you probably tolerate a lot of it in your life. You likely have friends who have snubbed you, but you don't feel the need to take serious action the way you would if you were physically threatened. Nor do you realize the extent to which you are potentially being seriously hurt when you go on social media and witness what you weren't a part of.

But stop and think for a moment. What if a friend walked up and punched you in the face? You probably wouldn't tell yourself, "Okay, that's fine. I should just take it and move on." You would feel pain and anger and would probably try to avoid that person in the future. But from the brain's point of view, being excluded and being punched in the face are not that dissimilar. The brain processes physical pain and social exclusion through overlapping distress circuits. This helps explain why being left out, rejected, or isolated can feel so profoundly painful.

Look at your life—you have likely allowed exclusion to fester in many of your dealings with others. If you understand the devastating effects that exclusion has on your psyche, and the pain you have been unknowingly inflicting upon yourself and others, you'll realize that you don't have to either inflict it or tolerate it. You can choose to avoid social pain, just as you would avoid situations where you're in danger of physical harm.

One of the reasons we seem to try to shrug off social pain (at least on the surface) is that our cultural norms allow it. When someone fails to invite us to an event they're hosting, even if we're hurt, we feel that we shouldn't let it get to us; it's not reasonable to expect that they will invite us to everything. The same goes for friends from school, meetings at the workplace, and the list goes on. That's why, even though these insights may strike you as true and important now, you're in danger of forgetting them in the weeks and months ahead.

For this reason, in the section below I've boiled this lesson down to three short points for you to review whenever you need a reminder.

## EXCLUSION CHEAT SHEET

Your brain experiences exclusion as highly aversive, affecting your very psychological core. Exclusion causes you to:

- feel you don't belong;
- feel less control over your life;
- feel a diminished sense of self-worth; and
- feel that life is less meaningful.

Don't let social norms that tolerate exclusion or rejection sway you. Join other social visionaries. Be inclusive and look for people who are inclusive of you.

If you are somewhat discouraged by finding out that you are exquisitely sensitive to exclusion, don't fret. It turns out that there's an easy antidote to exclusion, a way to protect your brain from its harmful effects and by doing so pave the road to long-lasting secure changes. The antidote is what I've come to call *hyperconnectedness*, which is the topic of the next chapter.

# 2

# A Life of CARRP: Fostering Hyperconnectedness

Imagine time traveling to the days when *Homo sapiens* were just another animal species in the middle of the food chain, not yet possessing language and other complex skills, vulnerable to attacks from predators, traveling across the African savanna hunting and gathering food. You have no house, no money, no real possessions except the few things you carry with you as you search for food. All you've got is your clan—the group of people you depend on and spend your life with. Now imagine that one day you suddenly lose track of them. Your heart will surely start pounding; you will cry out and run in different directions, trying to reestablish contact. Without the protection of your group, you become an easy target for the predators that abound.

We don't often think about life from the perspective of an animal in the middle of the food chain, but in many respects, our emotional brain still functions from that place. In that sense, having worldly possessions, such as condos or credit cards, is no guarantee of safety. What kept you alive on the savanna were the people you were close to. You would alert one another to potential danger and ward off predators together. In that setting, your level of connectedness to others was your most valuable asset. The more people you could depend on, the more social "capital" you possessed and the more secure you felt.

Mutual support isn't a prized asset only among humans. A study by Alexis Earl from Columbia University and colleagues observed that superb starlings—a hypersocial bird species living on the African savanna—form strong bonds not only with family but also with unrelated peers. Remarkably, unrelated starlings were seen feeding the chicks of their "friend" peers. On average, each starling had about five such friends, but some had up to sixteen helpers feeding their chicks. They didn't expect immediate reciprocity, either—these birds seemed to trust that help would come full circle in time. The researchers noted that in environments where resources were scarce, this kind of cooperation helped the entire flock survive.

Hyperconnectedness is sort of the reverse of the Cyberball experiment; now, two figures always pass the ball to the participant, and the participant passes the ball back to each of them in return—in essence, the par-

**A Life of Exclusion versus Hyperinclusion.** The classic Cyberball experiment, leading to exclusion, versus the reverse Cyberball experiment, leading to hyperinclusion.

ticipant is hyperincluded. Studies examining hyperconnectness find that it has immense benefits. The more the ball is tossed in your direction, the more in control of your life you feel. You develop a sense of belonging and even find that life is more meaningful. But it goes much further than that. Feeling connected has a profoundly positive impact on both body and mind, improving your memory, mood, and physical health.

## CONNECTEDNESS MAKES YOU SMARTER, HAPPIER, AND HEALTHIER

Becoming more secure by being connected can dramatically protect your brain on the most fundamental biological level. Two studies, by Joel Salinas from New York University and colleagues, and Isabelle van der Velpen from Erasmus University Medical Center and colleagues, examined whether there's a link between social support and brain volume and cognition. The studies found that the more connected people were, the greater their cognitive functioning and brain volume! Other findings suggest that socially cohesive societies promote happiness and well-being, even in the face of factors that may work against them. For example, despite its cold climate and somewhat limited resources, Iceland ranks among the happiest of nations year after year, even during economic downturns. Sociologists attribute this to the social cohesiveness of its people and the support they provide one another.

But sociability doesn't just affect the brain—it also affects the body. A multitude of studies have found a clear health benefit for people who are socially connected. Many of them show that connectedness provides a distinct protection against heart disease—the leading cause of death in the United States—and that, conversely, a lack of social connection can increase the risk more than being obese or having hypertension. And yet doctors don't typically relay this to their patients.

Social connection doesn't just protect you from heart disease. A meta-analysis by Julianne Holt-Lunstad from Brigham Young University and colleagues that combined 148 epidemiological studies examining roughly 300,000 people revealed that social connectedness has an overwhelming impact on longevity. It found an impressive 50 percent decrease in mortality risk for participants with stronger social ties. The survival advantage of social connectivity applied to everyone—it didn't matter your age, health status, or gender. No matter your circumstances, being connected helps you live longer.

Another remarkable study demonstrating the far-reaching effects of social connection on health was performed by Sheldon Cohen from Carnegie Mellon University and colleagues. The researchers intentionally exposed volunteers to the common cold virus and found that those who reported being more social and connected were less likely to fall ill. It seems as though their higher level of connectedness strengthened their immune system, helping them fight off the virus!

It turns out that connectedness is one of the most important factors in determining our health—in both body and mind. However, this potential for health and wellness comes with a caveat: As we discovered in chapter 1, aversive, exclusionary social experiences can have the opposite effect and be detrimental to our physical and mental health. The question, then, is, how do you promote social connectedness in your day-to-day life? How do you make sure the ball is tossed in your direction more often than not?

The answer is by creating a hyperconnected life.

## CARRP: THE FIVE PILLARS OF A SECURE, CONNECTED LIFE

If being hyperconnected is a surefire way to achieve happiness and live a long, meaningful life, how do we become so? It seems like such an elusive concept.

A LIFE OF CARRP: FOSTERING HYPERCONNECTEDNESS

For a long time, I searched for an answer, some simple yet effective way to become hyperconnected. It took some time, but in diving into our attachment and stress neurocircuitries, I've discovered a set of rules that, if followed, are sure to lead you to feel more connected and secure.

Surprisingly, I found that being connected from the brain's point of view is not so intangible, nor does it require that much work. Being connected doesn't mean you have to spend hours having heart-wrenching, soul-baring conversations. It also does not require being showered with gifts, or showering others with them, or being attached at the hip.

The brain neurocircuitry that determines whether you're safe is basically a surveillance system that scans the environment for the availability of people you have relationships with. It's like a radar that constantly monitors your surroundings for possible changes in connectedness. In essence, this neurocircuitry establishes an availability baseline for each person in your life. If it detects a change from that baseline, it triggers an alarm—the autonomic nervous system and related stress neurocircuitries—that compels you to engage in behaviors (known as protest behavior) to attempt to reconnect to the other person. If you're successful, all's well again; the system goes back to dormant mode and you go on with your life. If you're not successful, the system goes into overdrive, and you can become quite uncomfortable, even frantic. If the person remains unavailable to you despite your attempts to reestablish the connection, the neurocircuitry in your brain will eventually let go and you'll find yourself gradually thinking about them less and less or even starting to see them in a more realistic—and even negative—light. In attachment lingo, these are known as deactivating strategies.

How do you manage to keep your internal social surveillance system unperturbed?

It's easier than you might think. The trick is to avoid tripping the brain's connectedness alarm by paying attention to what I've come to call the five pillars of a secure life—consistency, availability, responsiveness, reliability, and predictability, or CARRP for short. Maintaining

CARRP in your interactions with others keeps your radar system and the radar systems of people you interact with from being tripped, allowing you to create a hyperconnected environment. You're creating a life in which you and the people around you are actively passing the ball back and forth to one another without any painful, brain-jarring interruptions.

Here is a brief breakdown of what it means to be CARRP.

## Consistent

Consistency is crucial for attachment security. A regular rhythm brings comfort—not just to babies but to adults as well. To stay connected, it's important to maintain a steady level of interaction with the people in your life. Once you've established a baseline, like calling once a day, once a week, or once a month, the attachment neurocircuitry becomes attuned to it. Any sudden change—like pulling back or going silent—can trip a physiological alarm.

## Available

You mentally make a decision to be there for the people in your life when they reach out. This means accepting a personal commitment to stay connected and to take some responsibility for their emotional and physical well-being. Without this decision, it's hard to follow through on the next part of CARRP: responsiveness.

## Responsive

Being responsive is the simple, practical outcome of being available. When people reach out to you, you respond as swiftly and consistently as you can. If you've fully committed yourself to being available, you find this action rather easy to do. It may even give you a sense of altruistic satisfaction. You are showing up for the people in your life. That's as noble as one can get from an attachment perspective.

You may think that you're CAR, but unless you receive an affirmation from the other person that they experience you as reliable and predictable, your work is not done. Being CARRP is not an individual experience. It's something that unfolds in the interaction between two people.

To be sure that you are indeed CAR, you must ascertain if you come across that way to another person. To verify CAR, you'll need to use a two-step authentication process and ask the other person if they experience you as someone who is *reliable* and *predictable*—in short, that you are CARRP.

Here's the breakdown of the two-step verification and the last two letters in the acronym.

### Reliable

Being reliable means that the other person feels that you're showing up for them in a consistent, available, and reliable (CAR) way. This cements your CAR behavior and teaches the attachment system that proximity will be maintained. It helps them feel secure that you won't disappear emotionally, flake out, or leave them guessing.

### Predictable

This is to make sure you don't surprise them with unpleasant ghosting experiences. You remain steadfast in your CARR commitment! The way you were yesterday is what they can expect you to be tomorrow.

*Predictable* can have a negative connotation in daily jargon. "He's so predictable," you might say, rolling your eyes about someone who never picks up his share of the tab. But make no mistake: From the perspective of your brain, especially within the context of CARRP, predictability is important in your quest to become more secure. Your attachment neurocircuitry, your radar for safety, gets tipped off by unpredictability, and to be secure, you want to keep this neurocircuitry at bay. You do this by making sure that you and others around you act in a predictable CAR way. You can still throw someone a surprise birthday party—that's great—but you can't go hot and cold on them without warning. Erratic availability is a surefire way to undermine your quest for hyperconnectedness and becoming more secure.

### The Five Pillars of a Secure Life

| | |
|---|---|
| **C**onsistent | You keep the same level of involvement over time without fluctuations. |
| **A**vailable | You are there for the other person when they need you. |
| **R**esponsive | When the other person contacts you, you respond. |
| **R**eliable | The other person feels they can count on you to be consistent, available, and responsive. |
| **P**redictable | The other person can anticipate your actions—no negative surprises like ghosting or other erratic or abrupt behavior and no stillfacing or Cyberballing. |

## BUILDING A SECURE VILLAGE

Setting yourself up with secure social connections is easier than you might think. You just need to follow the simple flowchart on page 35, and with time, you'll be able to finesse your social surroundings to the point where you will become primarily secure.

Start by taking inventory of your relationships. Make a list of the people in your life. Next, examine each one. Are they CARRP? If so, that's great. You can, and should, turn up the volume on your interactions with

## A LIFE OF CARRP: FOSTERING HYPERCONNECTEDNESS

them to form a hyperconnected social network and reap all the benefits I described earlier in the chapter.

But what about those in your life who aren't CARRP? Here's where you'll need to invest a little more effort by employing what I have come to call a *CARRP intervention*. A CARRP intervention is how you try to get people in your life to join your secure village. You approach them and share the importance of being CARRP in the hope that they can respond in kind. If you find that a friend consistently ignores your texts, you can ask them to be more responsive. If you feel that someone is excluding you from things, you can tell them you'd like to be included. Small, specific, and actionable interventions will help them understand how important being CARRP is in life and the simple steps they can take to join the CARRP revolution. This sometimes has a profound impact on people. It gives them a chance to find a secure core within them and start to express it in their own lives, too.

If your intervention worked, great! You've gained a CARRP enthusiast. Just give it a little time to make sure they're consistent in this new approach before allowing them a permanent home in your secure village. But if the intervention didn't work, you'll need to turn down the volume on your interactions with them and put the relationship on the back burner so they don't get priority in your life. That should be relatively easy to do if you're busy giving lots of attention to all the CARRP people whom you previously overlooked because so much energy went into those who weren't CARRP.

Sometimes you have key people in your life who are not CARRP, and you have no choice but to stay engaged with them. They might be a parent, a child, a sibling, a coworker, or anyone else you simply can't walk away from. Here's where you need to call upon some attachment shrewdness and creativity to generate a version of CARRP that will work in your specific relationship. This is what Michelle did with her two college-age kids.

Michelle used to reach out to both her kids, only to be ignored or met with annoyance. It hurt—deeply. She'd given her all to these children, and now that they were out of the house, *this* was what she got in return?

Then she had an idea. If her kids were always on their phones, why not meet them there? She started a family group on their favorite digital platform and began sharing cute photos of the family dog and other light, fun content. She also linked up with them through a fitness app, where they could all see each other's activity.

It became a steady rhythm of daily connection: step counts, exercise routines—small glimpses into each other's lives—all without needing to say much.

Through this private group and shared tracking, Michelle created a sense of daily hyperconnection. She redefined their back-and-forth in a way that kept the thread of attachment intact.

She joked to her best friend that while people always complain about social media getting in the way of meaningful connection, for her, it had the opposite effect. She felt that it brought her closer to her kids, as she connected with them on a daily basis.

There were two other things Michelle did. She hardly ever initiated calls with her kids, because she knew they'd most likely ignore her, and it would hurt. And she made a point of being available during the times they usually liked to call. You might think she was being a wimp, but for her, it was about staying connected to her kids in a way that didn't activate her attachment system or leave her feeling rejected. She found a way to stay close without getting hurt.

Even though CARRP is a straightforward concept, putting it into practice can be more challenging if you have an insecure attachment style. If so, you'll find details of how to implement CARRP in your life in part 2 of the book. But for now, I want you to embrace CARRP as a way to forge a more secure stance in your day-to-day interactions. CARRP is, in essence, a secure way to bestow your attention on the important people in your life.

A LIFE OF CARRP: FOSTERING HYPERCONNECTEDNESS

Simone Weil, a French philosopher who is considered one of the most original and intense thinkers of the twentieth century, once said, "Attention is the rarest and purest form of generosity." I firmly believe that to be true. CARRP is a structured way to unleash this form of generosity in your daily life.

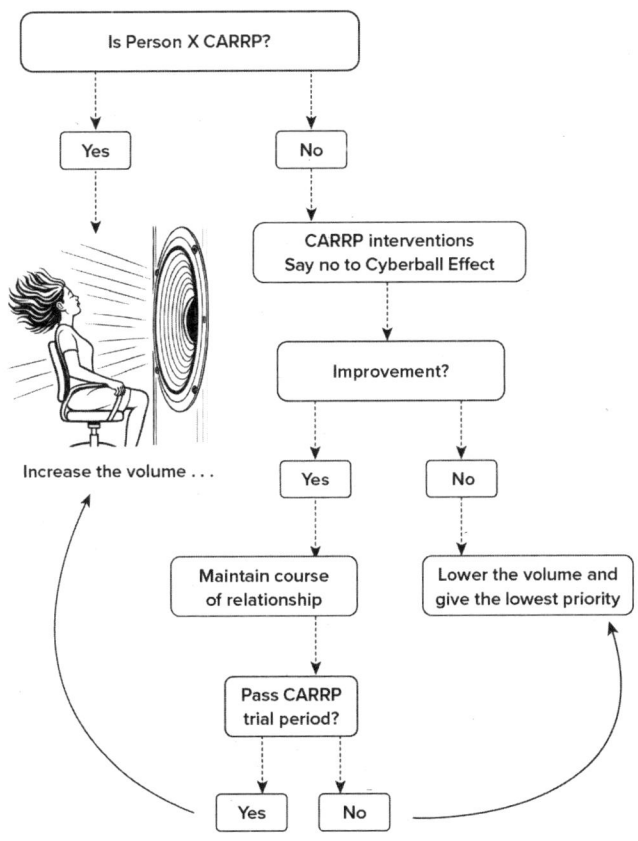

**Building a Secure Village Flowchart***

---

*CARRP = Consistent, Available, Responsive, Reliable, and Predictable

# 3

# Neuroplasticity: The Science (and Art) of SIMIs

## THE TRANSFORMATIVE EFFECT OF A SECURE ENVIRONMENT

In the last few decades, research in both animals and humans has shown that being immersed in an enriched, secure environment can provide a transformative healing effect. This was the kind of environment that Eric, a close friend and colleague, found himself in almost serendipitously.

Eric grew up with a very stern father who would chastise him for doing anything that he perceived as wrong—and there was plenty. For example, when Eric's mother enrolled him in an after-school program but he didn't like it and wanted to leave, a barrage of criticism ensued. His father would say, "You'll never amount to anything; you never finish what you start. You're good for nothing."

Eric was a naturally talented athlete who excelled in all forms of sport. But if he put on gym clothes or picked up a racket or a ball to play with friends, his father would mock him: "You're not really going to exercise.

It's just for show." Similar criticisms ensued about how he ordered food at a restaurant, or the way he spoke to his friends. Nothing escaped his father's scrutiny, and he would deliver a steady stream of disparaging remarks on an almost daily basis.

Eric's mother, while loving and supportive in general, seemed helpless in these moments, retreating into the background. "Don't antagonize him," she would tell Eric, as if wearing gym clothes were an antagonizing move. "But I'm not," Eric would retort, to no avail. No matter how often he talked to her about how hurtful her distancing was, every time his father was upset with him, she would end up giving Eric the cold shoulder so his father wouldn't get upset with her, too. While Eric was a vibrant and social kid and an excellent student, his father's demeaning remarks and his mother's distancing took a toll. As he grew older, Eric became less engaged with his friends and started pulling away from the sports he loved. In fact, when Eric got on the track field or basketball court, his father's mocking voice would echo in his head, and he would feel all the energy drain from his body. He would just sit there, frozen, unable to move.

When Eric was in college, a classmate of his started to go to therapy and found it so helpful that she convinced Eric to go as well. "You gotta see this woman. She's amazing," she said. Eric wasn't sure he even needed therapy, but he was curious enough to give it a try.

Deborah was a retired university professor who became a therapist later in life, after she recovered from cancer. Eric was initially suspicious and cautious in the treatment, but that soon changed. Deborah was caring and warm. There was something disarming about her that won Eric over. Even though she shared the kindness and intelligence his mother had, unlike his mom, she was strong, grounded, and determined, unwilling to let anyone dictate her actions or decisions. Unwaveringly protective, she would encourage Eric to call if something was amiss. "Why should you be alone with difficult feelings," she said, "if you can call me and we can talk for five minutes and you can feel better?" He recounted his father's motto—how you should only count on yourself and not depend on anyone else—and she waved it away with her hand. "Oh, what nonsense," she said. "We live in a human society; our whole existence depends on trust and cooperation." When he had trouble exercising, Deborah was there. "Why should you jog alone? I'll join you in our next session," she said, and indeed she did: They ran together. She seamlessly integrated a behavioral approach to help Eric overcome an emotional barrier he had struggled with for years.

Slowly but surely, Eric began to change. From being calculated and on guard with people around him, he began to let go and act more freely and naturally. His relationships deepened, he was able to silence the harsh voice he'd adopted from his father when speaking to himself, and he felt more content. He attributes to Deborah his success in life, his peace of mind, and his renewed appreciation of himself, as well as a newfound love for any exercise: Gym, swimming, running, biking—you name it, he does it, no longer held back by disparaging voices.

Without knowing much about neuroscience, Deborah, a naturally talented therapist, intuitively understood that the therapeutic hour might not be enough to create a drastic change in the brain. Instead, she surrounded Eric with a secure, enriched environment, instructing him to call her if he was feeling down so she could be there to help, even going running with him to overcome a psychological obstacle that stood in his way. The secure, nurturing environment Deborah provided helped Eric transform his brain—he went from being a cautious and suspicious person to an open and loving one.

## THE MALLEABLE SOCIAL BRAIN

The human species is one of the most adaptable on earth. We can inhabit almost any ecological niche on the planet, from the Sahara to the North Pole. We can even set foot on the moon, not by virtue of our physiological prowess but by virtue of our ability to form highly complex social connections and cooperate to find ways to survive in even the harshest of climates. One striking example is the global eradication of smallpox—a devastating illness estimated to have claimed 500 million lives worldwide and contributed to the destruction of many Indigenous communities. Through an unprecedented international effort spanning decades, health workers crossed borders, war zones, and language barriers to vaccinate entire populations. In 1980, the World Health Organization declared smallpox eradicated—the first and only human disease we've successfully wiped off the face of the earth.

In his book *Sapiens*, which describes the history of the ascent of human civilization, Yuval Noah Harari posits that we became the dominant species we are today because of our unmatched ability to collaborate in large groups and create complex social institutions. From a neuroscience perspective, given that collaboration is our main source of strength, we have evolved to have an intricate repertoire of social interactions and developed social neurocircuitries that are far more versatile and complex than most people realize. Our neural networks constantly respond and adapt to our ever-changing social situations, and our daily social interactions continue to mold and change our brains, reshaping who we are on a fundamental biological level.

As we discussed in chapter 2, positive social experiences are hugely beneficial to our bodies as well. Studies show that people who receive social recognition, like Nobel laureates and Olympic medalists, tend to live longer.

The good news is that you don't need to be an Olympic medalist or a Nobel Prize winner to gain these benefits. Close, supportive relationships can have a profound impact on your health and longevity. And even if you've faced adversity in your life, as Eric did with his father, your brain can still change and heal when you're immersed in a secure environment.

But there's a caveat. It takes time to convince the brain that the environment has changed—especially if those early experiences were particularly harsh or lacking. For example, several studies in rodents show that rat mothers differ in how they care for their pups. Some are "high licking and grooming" mothers, frequently tending to their pups, while others lick and groom far less. These mothering styles shape the pups' behavior. Pups raised by high-licking-and-grooming mothers grow up to be bolder, more curious, and less anxious. They also tend to become high-licking-and-grooming mothers themselves. In contrast, pups raised by low-licking-and-grooming mothers are more timid and anxious, and as adults, the females tend to repeat that same low-care pattern with their pups.

What's remarkable is that this difference traces back to changes in the brain. In pups that are frequently groomed, certain molecular "tags"* are removed from the DNA in the hippocampus.† The removal increases the expression of glucocorticoid receptors, the brain's sensors for stress hormones. As a result, these rats grow up less anxious and more confident. Early life experiences, it turns out, literally leave a molecular stamp on the brain.

The question is, can this biology be changed later in life? Under the right conditions, it can. In one experiment, Debora Cutuli from Sapienza University of Rome and colleagues took adolescent female rats that were destined to become low-licking-and-grooming mothers and placed them in an enriched environment—a sort of five-star rat hotel. These enclosures were spacious and stimulating, filled with toys and running wheels and other friendly female rats who huddled and groomed one another constantly. ("They were literally sleeping on top of each other and grooming and playing all day," one researcher told me.) After a month—a relatively long time in a rat's life—these future low-care mothers transformed. They showed an uptick of oxytocin-receptor density in their brains, in-

---

*DNA methylation, a kind of switch that binds to DNA and turns genes on or off.
†A brain region crucial for memory and learning and managing stress.

creasing their attachment proclivity, and when they became mothers, they engaged in high-licking-and-grooming behavior. What's more, their daughters did, too. The change persisted for generations.

So it turns out that if you provide the brain with the right ongoing conditions, it can overcome even childhood programming to become more secure. Studies additionally show that the right environment can lead to the birth of new neurons in the brains of rodents as well as of nonhuman primates, a phenomenon called neurogenesis. The trick for making the brain more secure? Immersion over prolonged periods of time in small but highly beneficial day-to-day interactions.

## THE SECURE ENVIRONMENT AND THE ART OF HEALING

Living in a secure environment has a powerful healing effect. This happened to Ava, a close family friend.

One August morning, Ava's husband collapsed on the floor. All attempts to resuscitate him, first by her and then by the EMS that quickly arrived at the scene, failed, and he was pronounced dead from what appeared to be a massive heart attack. For a long time, Ava couldn't comprehend it. One moment they were having breakfast, sipping coffee, and talking about the news, and the next, he was gone. Sometimes she would wake up and instinctively look over to her husband's side of the bed expecting to see him. Other times she thought she heard him coming up the driveway or walking softly about in the next room, only to remember that he was gone and sink into despair. She was full of sadness and anger and often just felt numb, disconnected from the world she had always known. Days went by without her doing much of anything. It didn't help that they lived in a small town where everyone knew them as a couple.

One day, Ava decided that she needed to change her environment if she was ever going to overcome her grief; she simply couldn't stay in their

# NEUROPLASTICITY: THE SCIENCE (AND ART) OF SIMIS

home anymore. She packed up and moved across the country to a quiet neighborhood lush with gardens and greenery. Each morning, she woke to the sound of birds chirping in the backyard and would lie in bed watching rays of sunlight peek through the trees.

After a few weeks, Ava decided to visit the nearby community center. A yoga class was about to start, and she surprised herself by joining. As she moved through the asanas with the others in the class, she found herself breathing into the challenge as the yoga teacher instructed. And it helped her feel a little better. At the end of the class, a group of women greeted her. No one knew her history; they didn't even ask. They were just nice for the sake of being nice, not because they felt sorry for her. It was a breath of fresh air.

They told her about other gym classes at the center that were worth attending and invited her to join them for lunch. She felt so welcomed and included. And that was just the beginning. Over the next few weeks, as she ventured out of her home more and more, Ava discovered the strangest thing. Everyone, literally everyone, she passed by waved hello and smiled at her. And it wasn't just pedestrians; people passing in their cars all waved hello, too. The first few times she was thrown off. She even looked behind her to see if they were waving at someone else. But she soon realized this was the norm here. Even complete strangers greeted you in this community. A little time went by, and then one morning she woke up and was struck by an unexpected feeling—a spontaneous sensation of unexplained well-being and joy.

Unbeknownst to her, Ava had created an enriched environment for herself that helped her overcome her grief and heal. If you pay close attention to Ava's story, you will see that her enriched environment consisted of many small interactions that on a day-to-day basis changed her life for the better. I've come to call these small interactions the seemingly insignificant minor interactions of everyday life, or SIMIs for short. What most people don't realize is that our SIMIs, the ones that often escape our attention because we believe they are of little consequence, are actually of huge importance in the process of changing your brain and your life toward greater security.

## THE SEEMINGLY INSIGNIFICANT MINOR INTERACTIONS OF EVERYDAY LIFE (SIMIs)

Oftentimes when people seek professional help to overcome emotional and social difficulties, they think of sifting through their early childhood experiences with a therapist as the main vehicle for healing and change. Seldom do people pay much attention to the minutiae of their day-to-day social interactions. But from the point of view of the brain, the minor interactions we have with people not in the past but in our present, everyday lives—whether close allies, significant others, friends and family, or even just colleagues, acquaintances, or passersby on the street—can be a powerful avenue to achieving radical transformation. Change can, in fact, come from taking command of the SIMIs of everyday life.

Neuroscience studies reveal that SIMIs have the potential to shape and reshape our brains countless times. They can either strengthen existing neurocircuitry or overwrite it to create new pathways. Positive SIMIs can provide us with the opportunity to heal past adversity as new experiences overwrite the old. But negative SIMIs can further solidify past relational experiences that did not serve us then and will not serve us now or in the future. Each positive SIMI is an opportunity for neuroplastic shift, which means that the right SIMIs have the potential to alter the brain on the most fundamental molecular level—helping you attain a richer, more satisfying life.

While most animals, driven primarily by instinct, have very limited control over whom they will interact with and how, human beings have a greater degree of freedom. In our society today, we don't have to stay at a certain company or in a certain job, nor do we have to stay in relationships—whether romantic, familial, or platonic—that are harmful to our brain. We can remove ourselves from one social milieu and try our luck in another. And we can try to change a certain dynamic within an already existing social context; this, if successful, can result in dramatic improvements in well-being and happiness.

## WHEN SIMIs AREN'T CARRP: THE THERAPY THAT WASN'T THERAPEUTIC

Gerry came to see me to learn Secure Priming Therapy. During one of our supervision sessions, he recounted an experience he had had ten years earlier. Then a resident in psychiatry, Gerry had decided that he wanted to become a psychoanalyst, and so he was required to embark on his own analysis for at least a year, which meant going to therapy four times a week, lying on the couch, and talking about whatever came to mind.

Gerry went to see a renowned and well-respected analyst whose office was situated in a prestigious building on Park Avenue on the Upper East Side in Manhattan. Each day of the week, excluding Fridays, Gerry had to be quick with his tasks at the hospital on the West Side so he could leave early enough to take the subway downtown and then catch the crowded crosstown bus to get to the East Side on time.

In session with me, Gerry shared that one detail about this analyst's behavior drove him to distraction. Gerry shuffled uncomfortably in his chair, hesitating for several moments before telling me that the renowned analyst would not take the classic ten-minute on-the-hour break between patients but instead piled the sessions on top of one another. This meant that he was invariably several minutes late for his sessions with Gerry. When he was on time, it was at the expense of the patient before. Inevitably Gerry or someone else got the short end of the stick.

When Gerry told the analyst that he found his constant lateness unsettling, the analyst dismissed him with a sweeping hand gesture. "Oh, what of it?" he said. "My therapy sessions extend for *about* forty-five minutes; sometimes they're a little more than forty-five minutes and other times a little less, but it's just a few minutes here and there. In the end, it evens out."

But for Gerry, it was much too much. It weighed on him as he raced through the day in order to leave early enough to make it to his session on time, only to find himself sitting in the waiting room, wondering how late his therapist would be this time. And this happened nearly every session. Eventually, he stopped seeing the analyst and decided not to pursue analytic training.

In supervision, Gerry and I discussed how the analyst had failed to provide all of the basic CARRP pillars of security. Even though the analyst was late by just a few minutes each time, it still mattered. He wasn't consistently available, nor was he reliable, and the session start time was unpredictable. In addition, when Gerry brought it up with him (which was essentially a CARRP intervention), he failed to be responsive as well.

Gerry's analyst had also ignored a cardinal rule of psychotherapy regarding the therapeutic frame. As far back as Sigmund Freud, there has always been an emphasis on creating a safe therapeutic space for patients, beginning with a session framework that emphasizes consistency and punctuality. Without this, Freud argued, the treatment would be of little use. Even though Freud didn't know the neuroscience behind SIMIs, and attachment science emerged only after his time, he and his students intuited with their sharp clinical understanding and skill the importance of CARRP SIMIs for the well-being of the patient's brain. In our sessions, I made every effort to be consistently on time. This allowed Gerry to experience secure, CARRP SIMIs that counteracted his earlier negative experience, which had festered in his mind since residency. He has since used the same positive SIMIs to create a safe therapeutic space—a secure base—for his patients as well.

# NEUROPLASTICITY: THE SCIENCE (AND ART) OF SIMIS

Even something as small as being right on time or giving a nod of acknowledgment matters to the brain. This is actually great news because we can achieve a large impact by introducing small positive SIMIs to our lives.

> **OPPORTUNITIES FOR SECURE SIMIs ARE ALL AROUND US**
>
> You, too, can take advantage of the secure SIMIs all around you to enrich your social environment. Think of these SIMIs as hidden gems scattered throughout your day—small, meaningful moments waiting to be uncovered. A SIMI could be found anywhere: It might be the person you run into in the elevator on your way to work, the barista at your favorite coffee shop, or even the customer service rep you talk to on the phone. Just a simple nod of hello can be enough, or a kind tone over the phone. By acknowledging the people around you, you enrich both your life and theirs—helping to carry the secure revolution forward. And if they don't respond in kind? No matter. You register a small setback, take it in stride, and move on to the next one who will. Not everyone is on board with the SIMIs revolution yet. Regardless, positive SIMIs are a way to get your daily dose of hyperconnectedness to boost your self-esteem. They give you the feeling that life is meaningful as well as a greater sense of control over your life, as we saw in chapter 2.

## SECURE SIMIs CAN HELP THE BRAIN AT ANY AGE

In 1949, Donald Hebb, one of the founders of the field of neurobiology, noticed that rats that he occasionally brought home for his kids to play with and then returned to the lab performed better in cognitive tasks, such as mastering a maze to find a food reward. He attributed this to the fact that the stimulation at home with his kids, in contrast to the rats' mundane life in a cage in the lab, improved the animals' memory and learning. This was one of the first mentions of what was later dubbed *environmental enrichment*: the fact that certain types of environments can be advantageous to the brain.

Since Hebb's observation, multiple studies of various species, including humans, have revealed similar findings, and this has sparked a whole modern approach to raising children that emphasizes providing them with rich stimuli to promote brain development. While it was initially believed that such environmental enrichment was important during critical periods of child development, and that once individuals reached adulthood the brain was essentially fixed, with very little change possible, more recent research reveals that enriched environments can alter the brain in beneficial ways in adulthood as well.

Enrichment doesn't have to be limited to social interaction. It can also come from taking on new challenges that stimulate the brain, such as learning a new skill. In experiments where research subjects were taught to juggle, both adolescents and senior citizens showed an increase in gray matter in specific areas of the brain that are related to movement, learning, and memory. True, the young people were much more dexterous and learned to juggle more proficiently, but senior citizens also learned, albeit more slowly. Most important, being involved in the study and learning to juggle provided the senior citizens an enriched environment that brought about positive changes in their brains!

This demonstrates that enrichment continues to reshape the brain well into adulthood. And when that enrichment comes through our social world—in the form of secure, supportive connections—the effects can be even more profound. In fact, research by Nathan Hudson from Southern Methodist University and colleagues shows that even just learning about attachment styles and secure traits can gradually help adults become more secure over time.

# NEUROPLASTICITY: THE SCIENCE (AND ART) OF SIMIS

## CREATING SECURE SIMIs

How do you create SIMIs that benefit your brain and your life? If you have already begun to say no to the Cyberball effect and say yes to CARRP, you're well on your way.

The most important message I hope you'll take away from this first part of the book is that by changing your social milieu, you can change your brain and improve your life. You can create your own "socially enriched environment" in which you go through daily life feeling safe and secure. The tools you'll find throughout this book will help you remove potential insecure obstacles and develop greater security, one SIMI at a time. You can start right now by doing the following:

1. Be aware of the *Cyberball effect* and its deleterious impact on your brain.

2. Practice the antidote for exclusion: a life of *CARRP* that will create a hyperinclusive and hyperconnected environment for you to thrive in. *Hyperconnectedness* helps you feel that life has meaning, provides you with a sense of control over your life, and boosts your self-esteem.

3. With the Cyberball effect and CARRP in mind, become attuned to the *seemingly insignificant minor interactions (SIMIs)* in your daily life. Reshape you brain and your life toward greater security, one SIMI at a time.

PART II

# Living in Secure Mode

Think about what you would do if something bad happened to you. Say you receive some upsetting news or get physically hurt in some way. You likely immediately have an idea of whom you will reach out to for comfort and, if they're unavailable, the next person, and the one after that. And quite often, when you talk to one of these people, or even just hug them, you feel better.

This is living in secure mode. You are able to find quick solace because one of the most powerful ways of handling emotional distress is by being close to a person you are securely connected to. There's no Xanax or Klonopin in the world that can come close to the immediate and profound effect of a secure connection. That's because we're a social species, and being in the presence of trusted others is a fundamental way to regulate our emotions and to feel safe.

But there's a caveat: When relationships involve insecure attachment patterns, they can be one of the most powerful generators of emotional distress. A perceived slight from someone can easily make you upset and upend your day. So our attachments can be both the cause of suffering and the antidote to it. The question that arises then is, how can you ensure that relationships are a healing force in your life rather than a destructive one?

In the course of my work over the past several years, I've discovered the unexpected answer. To make relationships a healing force in your life, you must ensure that they provide your brain with energy rather than sap it away.

When I use the word *energy*, I'm not using it metaphorically. I'm talking about real energy, on a cellular level in the brain. It turns out that the unique way in which your brain uses energy is directly connected to your quest to become more secure. The following chapter is devoted to this issue.

The rest of part 2 explores each insecure attachment style—anxious, avoidant, and fearful avoidant—and offers tailored tools and interventions to help move toward secure mode. These chapters are for everyone, because even if you're mostly secure, we all have moments of insecurity and we all interact with people whose styles differ from our own. Understanding these patterns, and learning how to counteract them, helps you save energy on frustrating dynamics and invest more of it in connection and growth.

# 4

# Harnessing Your Brain's Energy to Maximize Your Potential

We often find ourselves swept up by difficult emotions with very little say in the matter. We worry about things or obsess over our own and other people's behavior. "Why did I do that? Why can't I do better? Why am I not living up to my potential?" Or "They've been unfair. They dismissed me. I'll show them." It can go the other way, too—you can get caught in compulsive self-reliance, repeating the idea that you don't need anyone, that you're fine on your own, that other people are just too much work. The list is endless.

As a therapist, I'm entrusted with helping my patients find a way to resolve these emotions so they can achieve greater contentment. I find that my patients' struggles often share one common denominator: They all require large amounts of mental energy that's difficult to rein in. As you'll see in this chapter, this energy is indispensable—and when freed up, it can be funneled toward more meaningful and enjoyable endeavors, bringing about greater productivity and contentment.

Over the years, I've come to realize that the way our brain uses energy is directly tied to our attachment wiring. People with secure attachment are like five-star energy-efficient systems—they know how to channel their brain's energy in a focused, balanced way. In contrast, people with insecure attachment tend to use their brain very inefficiently. Some burn through energy on constant vigilance and worry, while others spend just as much energy suppressing their relational needs and overemphasizing independence. So how can we switch from insecure to secure mode and free up this precious energy?

Meditation and mindfulness techniques are often recommended, and these may be helpful. But I have discovered that there's another unexpected yet powerful way to attain this goal. It has to do with how the human brain uses energy, and how we can help it do so more efficiently and help you become more secure.

To do that, we'll first need to understand how the brain consumes energy by diving into its inner workings—down to the level of individual neurons—and how they use energy to make us who we are.

## EMOTIONAL ENERGY TAKES UP A TREMENDOUS AMOUNT OF REAL ENERGY

In the 2014 movie *Lucy*, starring Scarlett Johansson and Morgan Freeman, Freeman, portraying a renowned university professor, addresses an auditorium of students and says with impressive authority, "It is estimated most human beings only use ten percent of their brain's capacity.... Imagine if we could access a hundred percent." The movie then follows Johansson's character, Lucy, who, due to an accidental drug exposure, is able to use her brain's full potential and by doing so gains the ability to bend the laws of physics.

While the idea that we use only a small portion of our brain captures our imagination, and is certainly greatly entertaining in *Lucy*, it's a myth that has been perpetuated for decades in popular culture. The truth is that you use a good portion of your brain all the time; in fact, the brain's energy use is humongous, almost insatiable.

It starts with the fact that all life, beginning with cellular life, requires a lot of energy. That's not a metaphor; it's a factual description. All living cells (and we humans are essentially a lump of many cells bundled together) have an electric charge that lies across their membranes. This charge is called a resting potential, and it's typically a static, nonvarying charge that ranges from about negative forty to negative ninety millivolts.

Maintaining this resting potential requires a constant supply of energy. Tiny pumps in the cell membrane work tirelessly, 24/7, to drive two potassium ions into our cells and remove three sodium ions in exchange, creating an imbalance that leads to a negative charge inside the cell. To power this process, these pumps rely on adenosine triphosphate (ATP)—the cell's energy source. That means even maintaining a "resting" potential requires the cell to constantly burn fuel just to hold this baseline, which is a hallmark of life. Think of it like tirelessly bailing water out of a leaky boat to stay afloat.

Brain cells, or neurons, have evolved to do more than just have a resting potential—they can change the charges along their membrane and create an *action potential*. When this happens, a rush of sodium ions enters the cell, flipping the charge at a single point across the membrane, which then triggers an electrical current that flows through the neuron like a row of dominoes tumbling from a single push. Action potentials, the key element that enables the creation of a nervous system, were a foundational evolutionary breakthrough that allowed ultrafast communication among cells in the body. With action potential, conglomerations of cells can function collaboratively and form larger, more complex multicell forms of life, such as you and me.

Wiggle your big toe. Were you successful? If so, that means a multitude of action potentials took place to make it so, starting with reading this and interpreting the command and ending with sending an ultrafast signal from the brain's motor cortex, situated at the front of your head, all the way down to your big toe to initiate the movement. The fact that you can do this is nothing short of astounding, if you stop to think about the biological ingenuity that had to go into making this simple movement possible. To make things even more complicated, the message doesn't go straight from your brain to your toe; it stops along the way at certain relay junctures, called synapses, which are little gaps between neurons where the electrical charge cannot cross. Here the message continues to travel through neurotransmitters—chemicals that are discharged into the synapses to continue the message along. These chemicals are released, absorbed, and dismantled constantly, even as you're reading this.

But there's a caveat. Action potentials and synaptic transmissions come with a hefty energetic price tag. Imagine constantly tidying your house to make it nice and neat, only to have big waves come through and mess it all up as soon as you're done. Each time, you try to quickly put things back in place, only to have it all undone again and again. Think how much work that would be. Now imagine doing that 24/7, because that's what the brain does. Action potentials are happening around the clock, even in your sleep. They never stop. This continual activity turns the brain into a formidable energy guzzler. Even though the brain makes up only 2 percent of your body weight, it uses about 20 percent of the body's glucose and 15 to 20 percent of the body's blood flow, thanks in large part to action potentials! And there's more....

Neurons, the energy guzzlers, are such demanding, entitled cells that they don't even bother having their own place to store energy, the way most cells do. They're too big and important to manage a storage facility. Instead, they rely exclusively on an ongoing, immediate supply of glucose (or ketones, an alternative fuel source when glucose is low) to make ATP to ensure continuous functioning. This dependence comes at a steep price: The reliance on rapid, uninterrupted glucose and oxygen delivery makes the brain one of the most vulnerable organs in the body.

Take a look at the chart on the next page. You can see that without a continuous supply of sustenance, the brain will falter within several minutes, while other tissues can remain viable much longer thanks to their ability to minimize their energy requirement and to store energy.

**Tissue Survival Time When Oxygen Is Cut Off*** 

| TISSUE | SURVIVAL TIME |
|---|---|
| Brain | Less than 3 minutes |
| Kidney and liver | 15–20 minutes |
| Skeletal muscle | 60–90 minutes |
| Smooth muscle | 24–72 hours |
| Hair and nails | Several days |

## YOUR BRAIN AND ENERGY: INCREASING DEMAND, UNCHANGING SUPPLY

Then there's an added complication: What happens when the brain suddenly needs more energy?

This need for additional energy is not unusual for various organs and tissues in the body. When you exercise, your muscles send a message: "Hey, I'm working harder here; I need more energy"—and, in turn, blood vessels expand to increase blood flow to your muscles. When you eat, your gut needs more energy to digest the food, so blood flow increases there, too, by up to 200 percent! But how does the brain cope when it needs to work harder and therefore requires additional energy? Say you're studying

---

*R. M. Leach and D. F. Treacher, "Oxygen Transport-2: Tissue Hypoxia," *British Medical Journal* 317, no. 7169 (November 14, 1998): 1370–73.

for an exam, or you have an important project at work, or you have a new baby, and you want to perform at peak capacity. Can the brain just increase its blood flow to meet these increasing demands?

The answer is no. The brain doesn't have this option. You can't increase blood flow because the brain, a soft, mostly fatty tissue, is enclosed in the skull—it can't expand. Without room to swell, it must make do with a finite amount of blood flow and energy. Any increase in blood flow would cause the pressure inside the skull to mount instantly, leading capillaries to burst and the brain to hemorrhage. When blood flow decreases, not enough energy reaches the brain and neurons die within minutes, leading to a stroke.

This leaves your brain with a challenge: how to meet varying energy demands with an unchanging energy supply.

The best your brain can do is divert a little energy from one area to another, keeping some areas more activated than others. This is what you see in functional MRI studies: the brain parsing out its energy—glucose—to different regions depending on need. The differences in which regions are more activated than others might be small, but make no mistake: They can have an enormous impact on your life. If the amygdala, the part of the brain that alerts you to potential danger, is activated more often, you will experience frequent bouts of worry, fear, and anxiety. If the nucleus accumbens, the reward center of your brain, trumps the amygdala, it may drive you to engage in risky behavior and ignore the perils of your hedonic endeavors. The activation levels of different regions of your brain shape your daily life, steering your emotions, thoughts, behavior, and worldview.

## FREEING UP BRAIN ENERGY TO EXCEL

By understanding how energy works in the brain, we can start to use it more wisely. The brain has a limited energy budget, and much of that energy must go toward immediate survival—keeping you breathing, awake, and continuously scanning the environment to make sure you're safe. Even as you read this, part of your brain is monitoring for potential threats. If you suddenly heard a loud thud or saw something move out of the corner of your eye, you'd stop reading to assess whether you were in danger.

One of the most energy-hungry parts of the brain is the prefrontal cortex—the region responsible for abstract thinking, creativity, planning, and self-reflection. Its neurons are large and metabolically demanding. Because of this, the brain grants only limited access to this prized area. You can't spend all day pondering the meaning of life or strategizing your next big idea. That energy is carefully rationed, with much of it reserved for the systems that handle basic survival.

So how can you make sure you have more consistent access to these higher cortical areas—the ones that allow you to think abstractly, create, and plan your future?

## HOW THE BRAIN SAVES ENERGY

Say your brain is the secretary of the treasury. It wants to allocate resources to improving education and boosting innovation—but you're working within tight budget constraints. How do you achieve that without compromising your country's security? One solution is to curb military spending—but that carries obvious risks. A better strategy might be to form alliances with other nations and share the burden and cost of defense.

This is exactly what the brain does. It monitors for the presence of others around you in order to give you a sense of safety in numbers. In other words, it *crowdsources your safety*. This tactic isn't unique to humans; it evolved in the brains of many social animals millions of years ago, a brilliant scheme to help animals feel safer. The brain's ability to crowdsource its safety was an evolutionary breakthrough. Creatures that couldn't relax their vigilance because they lacked this built-in crowdsourcing security system were at a major disadvantage. They had to stay constantly alert, leaving them with little time to search for food, reproduce, or even just rest. You can feel this neurocircuitry firsthand. Imagine being alone in a dark alley versus having others nearby. You'd feel far more anxious alone. That's your crowdsourcing safety circuitry at work.

Some of the most eye-opening research on the brain's safety crowdsourcing neurocircuitry was done on several species of social birds. Most birds spend a good part of their lives in search of food—they hop around pecking at the ground for seeds and worms while frequently turning an anxious gaze upward to monitor for predators that might be swooping in. Observational studies of social birds reveal that when these birds are alone, they tend to shift their gaze upward a lot, constantly worrying they may end up as prey. But when they are in a group, this changes dramatically—the birds gaze up at the sky a lot less often. The neurons that sense others nearby signal to the neurons that monitor for threats to ease off, in effect freeing up neuronal energy to focus on other endeavors.

If you think about it, just having another bird by its side reduces a bird's chances of getting killed by a single predator by a whopping 50 percent—the predator will catch either that bird or the one next to it. And this doesn't even take into account the benefits of having other birds nearby that can alert the group to potential danger or come to the rescue, or that can teach new behaviors—such as how to use tools or avoid traps—all of which has been observed in the wild.

## YOUR BRAIN'S "SECURE SENSING" UPGRADE

The crowdsourcing neurocircuitry in humans comes with a crucial upgrade. Not only do humans have the capacity to sense the *number* of individuals around them and translate that to a greater feeling of safety, but they can simultaneously assess their level of safety based on the *quality* of those relationships.

Some of the most frequently referenced research in this area is experiments conducted by Jim Coan from the University of Virginia and colleagues. In these studies, the researchers asked participants to consider the potential threat of a mild electric shock while holding their partner's hand, while holding a stranger's hand, or while alone. They scanned the participants' brains with fMRI, which measures glucose consumption. Coan and his colleagues found that when participants were alone, brain areas related to threat detection and processing were most activated, burning more glucose. There was less activation when participants held a stranger's hand and the least activation when they held their partner's or a good friend's hand. Crucially, the more secure participants felt in their relationships, the less threat-related activation there was.

But it goes further than that. Your brain factors in the social environment even when assessing the difficulty of physical challenges. A study conducted by Simone Schnall from the University of Plymouth and colleagues found that when assessing the steepness of a hill, participants judged the slope as less steep if they were with a friend rather than alone. And the quality of the relationship mattered: Closer, warmer relationships were associated with lower steepness estimates. The take-home message is that the more trust and warmth you perceive in your relationships, the less daunting physical tasks seem.

As we can see from these studies, in real life, the secret to managing the brain's energy demands doesn't lie inside you. It may sound wild, but the findings make a convincing case that to increase the potential of our brain, we have to reach outside ourselves and get help from people around us. We can't do it alone.

When you are surrounded by people you feel really good about, your brain switches to secure mode and expends less energy on defensive vigilance, freeing up resources to love, work, create, and flourish.

## BRAIN ENERGY AND ATTACHMENT STYLES

If you have secure attachment, your brain operates in secure mode automatically. Research shows that in people who are secure, the amygdala is generally less reactive, and when it does become activated, they can calm it more easily. As someone with secure attachment, you may only need to shift your attention away from the situation that triggered the amygdala, and you're back to secure mode. If you have an anxious attachment style, your amygdala is easily activated by perceived relationship threats (for example, an angry expression on a friend's or partner's face) and it's harder to rein it in. In experiments where people with an anxious attachment style are told to think about and then stop thinking about a troubling relationship incident, their brains continue to activate areas that are associated with difficult emotions, and it's hard for them to quiet down this activation.

If you are avoidant, you spend a lot of brain energy suppressing the regions of the brain that typically react to relationship interactions. You also react less to both positive and negative relationship stimuli, so a smiling face—which would typically activate the reward area of the brain—doesn't register as much for you as it would for a secure person. This prevents you from utilizing positive relationship interactions, for instance, to find comfort from others when you might actually need it. It also means it is harder for you to access the crowdsourcing, energy-saving secure mode.

If you have an insecure attachment style, your brain—by virtue of your genes or your life experiences, or both—gravitates toward expending more energy on vigilance or self-reliance. If you score high in the avoidant or anxious dimension, or both (which you'll find out through the questionnaire in the next chapter), either you are often well aware of potential threats and can easily become preoccupied with them (the anxious dimension) or you spend a lot of time focusing on self-reliance (the avoidant dimension). Either way, you're not great at using others to help you save energy. If that's the case, it helps to give more careful consideration to reshaping your environment so that you can enter energy-saving secure mode. But reshape how?

The rest of part 2 is devoted to doing just that: helping each insecure style gain a deeper understanding of the benefits and challenges of your attachment orientation and how to use CARRP, SIMIs, and other tools to switch to secure mode. The goal is to lower your insecure shields by immersing you in an enriched, secure environment that will help you free up your energy.

In the next chapter, you'll need to determine where on the attachment spectrum you fall—that is, what your predominant attachment style is—so that you can use the tools in the way that's most beneficial to you.

## MAXIMIZING YOUR BRAIN'S POTENTIAL WORKSHOP

### "The War Against Math"

Leanora took her nine-year-old son, Nathan, to the doctor because he was bouncing off the walls. He could never sit still and had trouble focusing. He struggled in school, especially with homework. Every math assignment felt like a battle. He'd put it off; she'd remind him to do it. He'd say, "In a few minutes," and then an hour would go by. She'd remind him again. He'd try to sit down, but almost immediately he'd start fidgeting, looking around. It almost always ended with him in tears, frustrated and overwhelmed. And then, somehow, he'd sit down and fly through the whole thing in ten minutes, effortlessly. They used to call it "the war against math." It was waged every single time he had homework, and by the end of it, Leanora was completely drained—barely able to care for Nathan's six-month-old sister.

When she finally took him to the doctor, he diagnosed Nathan with ADHD and recommended Ritalin. But Nathan hated the medication. "I don't feel like myself on it," he told her. It also made him pick at his skin.

They tried a few other options; they all helped, but none was tolerable for long.

Then the doctor suggested two things: a rigorous athletic routine—as much exercise as possible—and something new to Leanora: a homework nanny. "They don't tutor the child," he explained. "They just sit next to them while they work. It's done wonders for some of the kids in my practice."

She decided to give it a try. They found Tich, a college student who Nathan immediately thought was cool. From the moment Tich sat down beside him, everything changed. Nathan was suddenly able to focus. He worked diligently and even began to excel. His teacher noticed the difference and started giving him extra problems to challenge him with more advanced material.

Circle the statement that best reflects what helped Nathan succeed with his homework:

1. Nathan's mom was controlling and overbearing, and it made his brain shut down. With her out of the way, his brain could finally focus, and he was able to get the work done.

2. After trying medication and experiencing side effects, Nathan got scared he'd be forced to take them again and started studying more.

3. Nathan doesn't have ADHD. He's just spoiled. Kids today just need more discipline.

4. Even though the medication wasn't a long-term solution, it showed Nathan he could focus and do well in math, which motivated him.

5. Having Tich sit beside him helped Nathan's brain perceive the task as less overwhelming, which allowed him to focus and succeed.

The correct answer is number 5. Because of his ADHD, Nathan naturally engages with his surroundings more than most people—looking around, fidgeting, darting from one thing to the next. So focusing takes more effort for him. Just like in the studies we reviewed in this chapter—where birds in groups could look up less and people judged a slope as less steep when standing next to a friend—when Tich sat beside him, Nathan's brain perceived the task as less daunting. The presence of someone he felt comfortable with gave his brain the extra energy boost it needed to focus. He was better able to concentrate, and the homework felt less effortful.

While Nathan's mom wasn't overbearing, the stress she carried—waging the battle over math homework (while also caring for a six-month-old)—didn't help activate Nathan's brain's crowdsourcing circuitry. He likely picked up on her tension, which may have made the task feel even harder.

## Crowdsourcing Challenge: Turning to Your Social Brain to Tackle a Daunting Task

Take a moment to think back on your life. Can you remember times when something felt easier—or even possible—because of your brain's crowdsourcing neurocircuitry?

For example:

- I remember running into the cold ocean in early spring while holding hands with Lila—the water felt less cold. I would never have gotten in if it weren't for her.
- I didn't think I could get through studying for my licensing exam. What really helped was being in the same room as Roy. We studied alongside each other. It was so much harder trying to do it alone.
- When it came time to move out of my dorm, I was frozen in place. I just lay in bed and couldn't make myself start packing. Then my mom video-called me, and while on the phone with her, I got up and did all the packing in two hours.

SECURE

Now write your own experiences.

_____
_____
_____
_____
_____
_____

What are the things you'd like to accomplish that the brain's crowd-sourcing neurocircuitry could help you with?

For example:

- I want to write.
- I want to exercise more.
- I want to organize my house.

_____
_____
_____
_____
_____
_____

List how you can use the brain's crowdsourcing neurocircuitry to help you achieve your goals. Write specific plans. Be creative.

For example:

- Have a friend join me when I have to take my dog to the groomer—it breaks my heart how he shakes and cries.
- Sign up with Miranda for a spin class that I've been eyeing.
- Invite Dan over to make the sourdough bread that I've been meaning to bake for ages.

_____

_____

_____

_____

_____

_____

## ENERGY AND YOUR BRAIN CHEAT SHEET

- Your brain has a finite amount of energy, which it must distribute across different brain regions.
- Which regions get more energy has a profound effect on your happiness and well-being.
- Secure relationships allow the brain to save energy it might otherwise expend on monitoring for safety, freeing it up for higher-level functioning so you can achieve more in life.
- Doing tasks with people you're securely attached to just feels easier, and you can use this brain energy hack to your advantage!

# 5

# Discover Your Attachment Style—in All Areas of Your Life

Imagine this: You are away on an important business trip, and when you get back, the first thing waiting for you is a message from your significant other. The message reads: "Call me when you get this, we need to talk."

What goes through your mind? Do you think they might have an exciting announcement, they got their big promotion, or they have great family news and are trying to get ahold of you? Or do you think they're upset with you, perhaps even planning to have the "breakup talk"? Maybe you don't think much of it at all and, because you're busy, you forget to reach out to them.

Similar scenarios happen with friends, family, and work colleagues. You get an email at work telling you to call your boss, or a friend tells you they can't make it to dinner. What goes through your mind?

Omri Gillath from the University of Kansas and colleagues posed a similar question to research participants, and they discovered that there's a pattern to how you will respond. Whatever your reaction might be, it is not by chance. You are responding according to predetermined programming that goes deep into the wiring of your brain—your attachment style.

## ATTACHMENT STYLES, DIMENSIONS, AND YOU

Your attachment style falls along a spectrum, determined by your position on two independent dimensions: anxiety and avoidance.

The *anxiety dimension* assesses the extent to which individuals worry about being abandoned or unloved. High scores on this dimension indicate a high level of attachment-related anxiety, characterized by a fear of rejection and a frequent need for reassurance.

The *avoidance dimension*, on the other hand, measures the degree to which individuals are uncomfortable with closeness and intimacy. High scores on this dimension reflect a high level of attachment-related avoidance, characterized by a strong desire for independence and discomfort with relying on others.

When people fear both rejection and closeness, they score high on both the anxious and avoidant dimensions and are known as *fearful avoidants*.

If you score low on both dimensions, you're secure. Your interactions with people around you require very little work; in fact, they help you conserve energy and use it more efficiently in your brain. The higher you score on the two dimensions, the more energy you have to spend on your relationships and the less energy you conserve.

The goal of part 2 is to give you strategies to crowdsource your safety and help you become more secure. You will discover specific tools for each insecure attachment style—anxious, avoidant, and fearful avoidant. But first let's assess where you fit along the attachment spectrum.

## HOW ATTACHMENT DIMENSIONS CAME TO BE

We've come a long way in deciphering attachment styles since psychologists Cindy Hazan and Phillip Shaver first introduced them in their groundbreaking 1987 paper, "Romantic Love Conceptualized as an Attachment Process." That study identified three categories of adult attachment styles—anxious, avoidant, and secure—based on a questionnaire they designed to assess participants' feelings and attitudes about their romantic relationships.

But that was just the beginning. Researchers in psychology are statistical wizards; they tend to prefer more nuanced ways of measuring certain traits than simply plopping people into one of several categories. As the field grew and became more recognized, the accuracy of measuring attachment in adulthood improved, too. In a breakthrough for the field, a new instrument to determine attachment styles was created: the Experiences in Close Relationships Scale, which was first published in 1998 by Kelly Brennan, Catherine Clark, and Phillip Shaver. Instead of fixed categories, this tool places people somewhere within four distinct quadrants by measuring high or low anxiety and high or low avoidance based on their scores. The assessment, which was further refined by R. Chris Fraley, Niels Waller, and Brennan in 2000, reflects the fact that how we experience relationships falls more on a spectrum than within a fixed category.

Designing a questionnaire with multiple precise measurements of the two dimensions pushed the field of adult attachment forward by leaps and bounds. It allowed researchers to closely examine and tease apart specific aspects of avoidance and anxiety in close relationships, leading to a deeper understanding of how people experience connection. But it achieved something even more impactful: It expanded adult attachment research beyond romantic relationships, enabling the study of attachment styles across all types of connections—with friends, coworkers, and family members—laying the groundwork for understanding how attachment plays out in every area of life.

This approach was solidified in 2011 when the Experiences in Close Relationships–Relationship Structures (ECR-RS) questionnaire was formally introduced by Fraley, from the University of Illinois, and colleagues. The ECR-RS allows you to assess attachment styles in a broad range of relationships beyond just romantic ones and gives you an idea of your attachment range and versatility.

What the researchers discovered is that while you may have a general attachment style that reflects your overall attitudes and beliefs about relationships, you can also develop specific—and even different—attachment patterns with particular people in your life.

This is both good and bad news. It means that even if you generally have an insecure attachment style, you can still develop secure relationships with specific individuals. But it also means that even if you're generally secure, some people can trigger insecure responses depending on what unfolds between you.

For example, you might have an anxious attachment style but experience secure relationship patterns with specific friends or colleagues. Or you may have an overall secure attachment style but find yourself responding more anxiously—or avoidantly—with a parent or sibling.

The key is to use the secure relationships as a vehicle for becoming more secure overall—and to be aware of the relationships that tend to bring out insecurity so they don't get in the way of your growth.

You'll now have the opportunity to complete Fraley and colleagues' ECR-RS. This is your first step in creating a personalized plan to become more secure.

DISCOVER YOUR ATTACHMENT STYLE—IN ALL AREAS OF YOUR LIFE

## ASSESSING YOUR ATTACHMENT STYLE: THE RELATIONSHIP STRUCTURES QUESTIONNAIRE*

This two-part questionnaire is designed to measure your attachment style in a range of relationships. In the first questionnaire, you will be asked to evaluate your general attachment style through a series of statements about your overall beliefs and attitudes toward relationships.

In the second questionnaire, you will be asked to assess your attachment style in specific relationships. You will respond to statements about your feelings and beliefs regarding people in your life, one person at a time. You can complete this questionnaire multiple times, each time focusing on a different individual: your parents, other family members, your significant other, a colleague or your boss, close friends, or anyone else you feel close to or spend a lot of time with.

To complete this questionnaire, arm yourself with a pencil and a calculator. It involves a bit of addition, division, and some simple graphing—but it's well worth the effort. In the end, you'll get a bird's-eye view of your attachment topography across your different relationships. You'll be able to identify patterns—both similarities and differences—and gain deeper insight into your strengths and areas for growth. This overall view will serve as a road map for the rest of part 2 in your quest to become more secure.

*Tip: For assistance with completing this questionnaire online—and to access additional attachment questionnaires—visit amirlevinemd.com.*

---

*Used with permission from R. C. Fraley based on: R. C. Fraley et al., "The Experiences in Close Relationships–Relationship Structures Questionnaire: A Method for Assessing Attachment Orientations Across Relationships," *Psychological Assessment* 23, no. 3 (September 2011): 615–25, doi: 10.1037/a0022898.

SECURE

## Deciphering Your General Attachment Style

### Instructions
For each of the following statements, circle the number that best reflects your level of agreement, using a scale from 1 (strongly disagree) to 7 (strongly agree). Be honest—there are no right or wrong answers.

### Rating Scale

1—Strongly disagree

2—Disagree

3—Slightly disagree

4—Neutral

5—Slightly agree

6—Agree

7—Strongly agree

Once you've circled your number for each statement, follow these steps to calculate your scores:

### Reverse Scoring Instructions
Some items (questions 1–4) that appear shaded are phrased in a way that requires reverse scoring. That means your answer needs to be converted before it can be added to your total. And there's an extra column to write down the reverse score there.

Use the following reverse-scoring key:

- 1 → 7
- 2 → 6

- 3 → 5
- 4 → 4
- 5 → 3
- 6 → 2
- 7 → 1

For example, if you selected 2 on question 3, your reverse score would be 6.

Questions 5–9 are scored as is—no conversion is needed.

### Scoring Each Item

After scoring all items (using the reverse scores where applicable), write the adjusted score for each item in the right-hand column.

Strongly Disagree     1   2   3   4   5   6   7     Strongly Agree

| QUESTION | RESPONSE SCALE | REVERSE SCORE 1→7; 2→6; 3→5; 4→4; 5→3; 6→2; 7→1 | FINAL SCORE |
|---|---|---|---|
| 1. It helps to turn to people in times of need. | 1 2 3 4 5 6 7 | | |
| 2. I usually discuss my problems and concerns with others. | 1 2 3 4 5 6 7 | | |
| 3. I talk things over with people. | 1 2 3 4 5 6 7 | | |
| 4. I find it easy to depend on others. | 1 2 3 4 5 6 7 | | |

## SECURE

**Strongly Disagree**    1   2   3   4   5   6   7    **Strongly Agree**

| QUESTION | RESPONSE SCALE | | FINAL SCORE |
|---|---|---|---|
| 5. I don't feel comfortable opening up to others. | 1 2 3 4 5 6 7 | | |
| 6. I prefer not to show others how I feel deep down. | 1 2 3 4 5 6 7 | | |
| 7. I often worry that other people do not really care for me. | 1 2 3 4 5 6 7 | | |
| 8. I'm afraid that other people may abandon me. | 1 2 3 4 5 6 7 | | |
| 9. I worry that others won't care about me as much as I care about them. | 1 2 3 4 5 6 7 | | |

### Dimension Scores

Now that you've written your final scores in the right column, it's time to calculate your **dimension scores** and enter them into the chart on page 79.

- For your avoidance score:
    - Add the scores from questions **1–6**.
    - Write the total (sum) in the "Sum" column.
    - Copy that number into the "Formula" column, add the division sign (÷), and divide by six.
    - Calculate the result.

- Write the calculated average in the "Average Score" column in the same row.

- For your anxiety score:

  - Add the scores from questions **7–9**.

  - Write the total (sum) in the "Sum" column.

  - Copy that number into the "Formula" column, add the division sign (÷), and divide by three.

  - Calculate the result.

  - Write the calculated average in the "Average Score" column in the same row.

| SCORE TYPE | SUM | FORMULA | AVERAGE SCORE |
|---|---|---|---|
| Average Avoidance Score (X-Axis) | Sum of Questions 1–6 | (Sum of Qs 1–6) ÷ 6 | |
| Average Anxiety Score (Y-Axis) | Sum of Questions 7–9 | (Sum of Qs 7–9) ÷ 3 | |

## Deciphering Your Attachment Style with Specific People in Your Life

### Instructions

Please respond to the following questions about specific individuals in your life, such as a partner (past or present), family members, friends, colleagues, or anyone else you wish to determine your attachment style with.

Refer to the instructions in the general attachment style questionnaire about how to rate your responses.

## SECURE

**Strongly Disagree**    1   2   3   4   5   6   7    **Strongly Agree**

| QUESTION | RESPONSE SCALE | REVERSE SCORE 1→7; 2→6; 3→5; 4→4; 5→3; 6→2; 7→1 | FINAL SCORE |
|---|---|---|---|
| 1. It helps to turn to this person in times of need. | 1 2 3 4 5 6 7 | | |
| 2. I usually discuss my problems and concerns with this person. | 1 2 3 4 5 6 7 | | |
| 3. I talk things over with this person. | 1 2 3 4 5 6 7 | | |
| 4. I find it easy to depend on this person. | 1 2 3 4 5 6 7 | | |
| 5. I don't feel comfortable opening up to this person. | 1 2 3 4 5 6 7 | | |
| 6. I prefer not to show this person how I feel deep down. | 1 2 3 4 5 6 7 | | |
| 7. I often worry that this person does not really care for me. | 1 2 3 4 5 6 7 | | |
| 8. I'm afraid that this person may abandon me. | 1 2 3 4 5 6 7 | | |
| 9. I worry that this person won't care about me as much as I care about them. | 1 2 3 4 5 6 7 | | |

# DISCOVER YOUR ATTACHMENT STYLE—IN ALL AREAS OF YOUR LIFE

Now that you've written your final scores in the right column, it's time to calculate your **dimension scores** and enter them into the chart below.

- For your avoidance score:
  - Add the scores from questions **1–6**.
  - Write the total (sum) in the "Sum" column.
  - Copy that number into the "Formula" column, add the division sign (÷), and divide by six.
  - Calculate the result.
  - Write the calculated average in the "Average Score" column on the same row.
- For your anxiety score:
  - Add the scores from questions **7–9**.
  - Write the total (sum) in the "Sum" column.
  - Copy that number into the "Formula" column, add the division sign (÷), and divide by three.
  - Calculate the result.
  - Write the calculated average in the "Average Score" column on the same row.

| SCORE TYPE | SUM | FORMULA | AVERAGE SCORE |
|---|---|---|---|
| Average Avoidance Score (X-Axis) | Sum of Questions 1–6 | (Sum of Qs 1–6) ÷ 6 | |
| | | | |
| Average Anxiety Score (Y-Axis) | Sum of Questions 7–9 | (Sum of Qs 7–9) ÷ 3 | |
| | | | |

## Plotting Your Attachment Topography

Now that you've filled out the Relationship Structures Questionnaire, it's time to plot your attachment topography as it relates to the important people in your life.

1. Plotting your scores on the graph
   - For the attachment evaluation, find the point where the calculated anxiety score (x-axis) and avoidance score (y-axis) intersect.
   - Mark this point on the graph on page 83.
   - Label each point clearly to indicate which relationship it represents.

2. Interpreting the graph
   - The position of each point will give you insight into the attachment style for that particular relationship.
   - Higher avoidance scores (farther up the y-axis) indicate greater avoidance.
   - Higher anxiety scores (farther right on the x-axis) indicate greater anxiety.

Once you've plotted all your scores, you'll gain a visual representation of your attachment style in different relationships. It may surprise you to find that your attachment can be versatile and malleable, responding and reshaping itself to adapt to different social situations. This is a key take-home message from this book. The trick is to create an environment that helps shape your attachment toward greater security.

*Additional tip: You can revisit this chart anytime to add new people to your attachment topography or to check whether your attachment style*

## DISCOVER YOUR ATTACHMENT STYLE—IN ALL AREAS OF YOUR LIFE

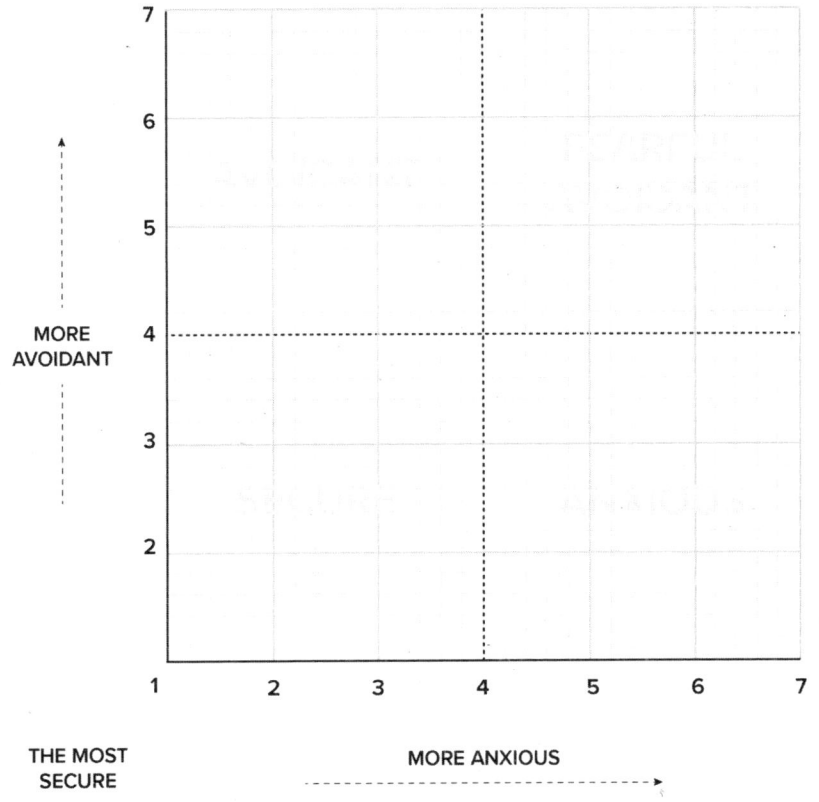

with a particular person has changed over time. A helpful way to track this is by using colored pencils—assign a different color to each person.

The following is a sample filled-in questionnaire.

## SECURE

**Strongly Disagree**  1  2  3  4  5  6  7  **Strongly Agree**

| QUESTION | RESPONSE SCALE | REVERSE SCORE<br>1→7; 2→6; 3→5; 4→4;<br>5→3; 6→2; 7→1 | FINAL SCORE |
|---|---|---|---|
| 1. It helps to turn to people in times of need. | 1 2 3 4 5 ⑥ 7 | 6 → 2 | 2 |
| 2. I usually discuss my problems and concerns with others. | 1 2 3 4 ⑤ 6 7 | 5 → 3 | 3 |
| 3. I talk things over with people. | 1 2 3 ④ 5 6 7 | 4 → 4 | 4 |
| 4. I find it easy to depend on others. | 1 2 3 4 5 6 ⑦ | 7 → 1 | 1 |
| 5. I don't feel comfortable opening up to others. | ① 2 3 4 5 6 7 |  | 1 |
| 6. I prefer not to show others how I feel deep down. | 1 ② 3 4 5 6 7 |  | 2 |
| 7. I often worry that other people do not really care for me. | 1 ② 3 4 5 6 7 |  | 2 |
| 8. I'm afraid that other people may abandon me. | 1 2 ③ 4 5 6 7 |  | 3 |
| 9. I worry that others won't care about me as much as I care about them. | 1 ② 3 4 5 6 7 |  | 2 |

## Attachment Style Average Scores

| SCORE TYPE | SUM | FORMULA | AVERAGE SCORE |
|---|---|---|---|
| Average Avoidance Score (X-Axis) | Sum of Questions 1–6<br>13 | (Sum of Qs 1–6) ÷ 6<br>13/6 = 2.16 | 2.2 |
| Average Anxiety Score (Y-Axis) | Sum of Questions 7–9<br>7 | (Sum of Qs 7–9) ÷ 3<br>7/3 = 2.33 | 2.3 |

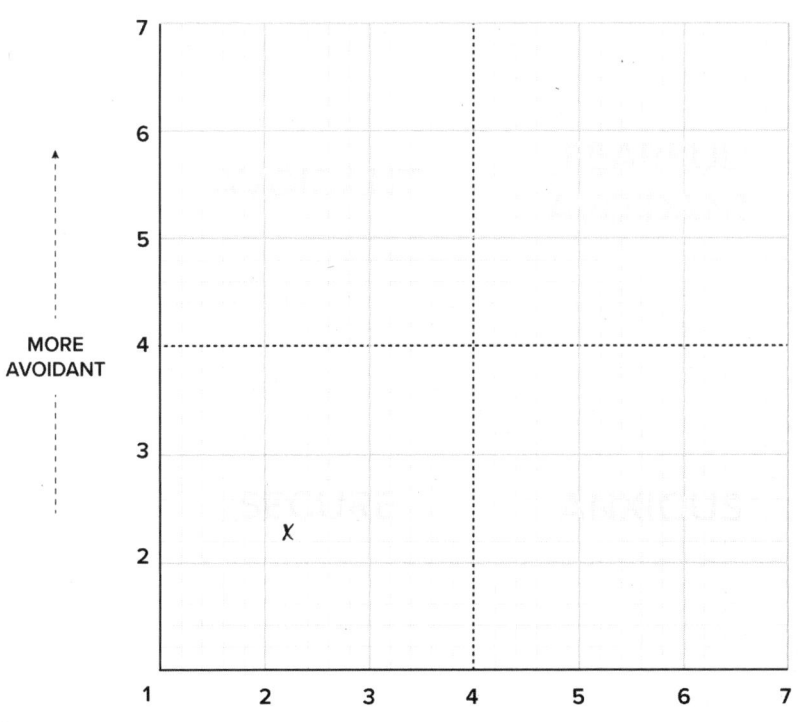

SECURE

## Attachment Interpretation

**QUADRANT 1: Secure attachment—low anxiety, low avoidance**
In many of your relationships, you tend to be warm and loving. You relish closeness, and you aren't easily threatened by the various relationship curveballs that life throws your way. You are often the last to know if someone is undermining you; you just don't see potential danger in relationships easily. That being said, in times when you do get upset, you're quick to forgive and quick to move on—and you're easily comforted and consoled.

**QUADRANT 2: Anxious attachment—high anxiety, low avoidance**
You have a low threshold for spotting potential relationship danger. Your radar is set in such a way that even the smallest blip will trigger the alarm. This heightened awareness can be extremely helpful when the environment is dangerous, as you will be able to spot potential threats before anyone else. However, if your surroundings are relatively safe, you tend to overshoot and sometimes register danger even where there is little of it. If you create an environment devoid of most threats, over time you can settle into a more secure routine, enjoy closeness with others, and for all intents and purposes feel secure. But make no mistake: You will still possess this special ability to spot things that others don't, and you will be able to put it to good use in every aspect of your life.

**QUADRANT 3: Avoidant attachment—low anxiety, high avoidance**
You highly value your independence and are mostly self-reliant. You often think about how to solve problems on your own rather than turning to anyone else for help. Your life philosophy is that everyone should be looking after their own well-being, and you don't particularly enjoy it when other people encroach upon you to fulfill their needs and wants. You take care of yourself, and they should take care of themselves, too. When it comes to closeness, you tend to feel uncomfortable with too much of it. You need to do things on your own time. You're like a stray cat—if people

want to get close to you, they need to put the milk out and you'll warm up to them when you're ready. They can't force it, because when they do, you instinctively retreat.

**QUADRANT 4: Fearful avoidant attachment—high anxiety, high avoidance**

You long for closeness, but you are also wary of its potential pitfalls. You usually find yourself on your own; relationships don't come easily to you. Like anxious attachers, you have a sensitive radar for danger; but unlike the anxious, who feel good about being close as long as there's no threat, to you, closeness itself can feel like a threat. Though you long for closeness, you proceed with such caution that you abandon even the prospect of potential relationships just to avoid possible heartache. In your existing relationships, you are easily hurt but also quick to push people away when they encroach on your space.

Most people find that while they tend to fall into one of the four quadrants in the general attachment questionnaire, their attachment style can vary significantly across specific relationships. This kind of flexibility is actually a strength—and you'll use it to your advantage as you learn to shape your environment into a more secure one.

## HOW ATTACHMENT DIMENSIONS PLAY OUT IN REAL LIFE

Let's return to the Gillath experiment from the beginning of the chapter. You've just returned from a business trip and received a message that says, "Call me, we need to talk." The findings show that people with secure attachment style are more likely to respond with a positive thought: A pleasant surprise is in store, your boss wants to congratulate you or offer a promotion, or a friend or family member has good news to share.

If you're avoidant, you are more likely to just ignore the request and "forget" to call altogether, or to think more along the lines of "They're too needy; I can't deal with them now. I just got back, so they will have to wait."

If you're anxious, you tend to see danger in relationships. You might assume your boss wants to fire you, your partner is about to break up with you, or your friends and family are upset with you.

If you're fearful avoidant, you might believe that the person is pulling away or about to end the relationship. But instead of calling and expressing how you feel, you may preemptively decide not to engage at all—avoiding what feels like an emotionally overwhelming conversation. You keep your distance while feeling deeply unhappy.

It's easy to see how the different ways of assessing the situation create different relationship outcomes. If you're secure, you call your partner while in good spirits, and that leads to easier, smoother interactions. If you're insecure—whether anxious, avoidant, or fearful avoidant—you respond in a way that is less than ideal. For example, when you call back, you may act cold or distant because you expect them to be upset with you; or you may not call at all, which leads to relationship tension and kicks the brain's surveillance neurocircuitry into overdrive—burning through a lot of energy.

## ATTACHMENT STYLES WORKSHOP

### Who's Right? The Birthday Party Argument

Jessica's husband, Andrew, received an invitation to his brother-in-law's birthday party. He showed it to Jessica and talked about whether they could make it. "You're not seriously considering going to that party, are you?" Jessica asked, shocked.

"Yes, why not?" Andrew asked.

"Well, I would ask, why *yes*?" she said. "After all that they've done to you? The way your sister treated you as a child, and how they made fun of you at dinner recently because they don't agree with your political views?

The whole table erupted in laughter at your expense, and you got upset. Don't you remember?"

"I remember," he replied, "but what of it? I left it there at the dinner table. I really didn't give it much thought afterward."

Which statement below is the most accurate?

1. Andrew is avoidant.

2. Jessica is anxious and Andrew is secure.

3. Jessica is anxious and Andrew is avoidant.

4. Both Jessica and Andrew are anxious.

5. None of the above.

The correct answer is 5, none of the above. It's important not to jump to conclusions when considering attachment styles. It's also important to think about where people fit along both the anxiety and the avoidance dimensions, not just one or the other. We don't have enough information to know if Andrew is avoidant or secure. What is clear is that he's not harping on negative interactions with his family to no end. So that eliminates the anxious domain—he'd score low there. Then we're left with one of two choices—avoidant or secure. He could be either—we don't know enough from the information presented here. He may defensively shut out awareness of negative events in the relationship and feel that self-reliance is key (i.e., score high on avoidance). Or he may not pay much attention to the negative interactions with his in-laws and appreciates closeness (i.e., score low on avoidance); if that's the case, he'd be secure.

Let me give you a little more information: Andrew proceeded to tell Jessica that he knows his family's not perfect, and he understands that his political views bother them. But they're important to him, and he loves them. After the dinner incident, he decided not to bring politics to the table anymore, knowing that this would make it easier for everyone to get along. He didn't want to give up on his sister and brother-in-law just because of their political differences. He said that he forgave his sister for mistreating him when he was a child. He acknowledged that he was not an easy child, which made it challenging for all of them.

Given this new information, which statement is the most accurate?

1. Jessica is low on the anxiety dimension.

2. Andrew is low in avoidance and low in anxiety.

3. Andrew is high on the avoidance dimension.

4. Jessica is low in anxiety and low in avoidance.

5. None of the above.

The correct answer is 2. Andrew is secure. He is low in avoidance and low in anxiety. Jessica scores high on the anxiety dimension; she sees danger in the way Andrew's family interacted with him. She may also score high on the avoidance dimension, since her solution is to avoid the situation altogether.

Who's right in this argument?

1. Jessica

2. Andrew

3. Neither

4. Both

The correct answer is 4—both. Each person has a valid point of view, because they experience the situation differently due to their attachment styles. Jessica, who's anxious, sees the danger in putting yourself in an environment where others will not respect your views or will try to put you down. And since she's more sensitive to potential relationship infractions, for her, it can really matter—she can really get hurt. Andrew, who's secure, is much less sensitive to such relationship dynamics. His attachment system doesn't register it as a threat ("Things got a bit out of control in the heat of the argument—it happens," he might think), so the chances that he'll get hurt are much lower. He justifiably sees the situation as less dire.

## Secure . . . and Anxious?

I received a text from a friend who had filled out the Relationship Structures Questionnaire. He sent me a screenshot of the results:

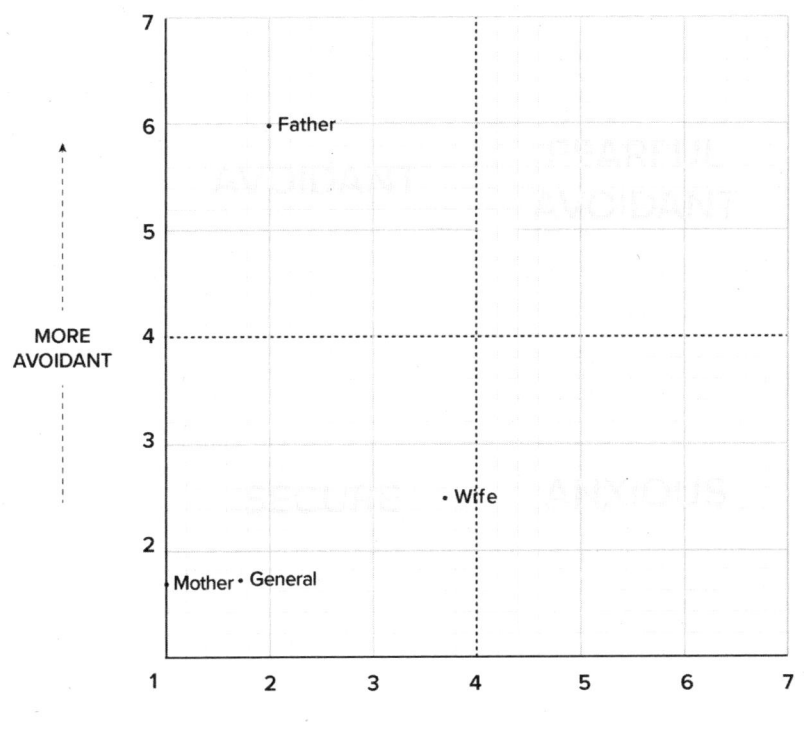

| | SCORE | |
|---|---|---|
| | Anxiety | Avoidance |
| Mother | 1 | 1.67 |
| Father | 2 | 6 |
| Wife | 3.67 | 2.5 |
| General | 1.67 | 1.67 |

Each score reflects how he interacts with important people in his life: his mom, his dad, and his wife. He scored his interactions with his dad as avoidant, those with his mom as secure, himself in general as secure, and his interactions with his wife as bordering on anxious. Which of the following statements are correct?

1. This person is all over the place. He filled out the questionnaire wrong.
2. This person correctly characterized his interactions with different important attachment figures in his life.
3. The fact that he's secure but his relationship with his wife borders on the anxious raises some questions about their interactions.
4. This person shows more anxiety with his wife, and since partner relationships carry the most weight in attachment, this pattern is what really counts.

Statements 2 and 3 are both correct. As I discussed in this chapter, we now know that attachment styles fall along a spectrum. In this case, my friend identified as quite secure in his interactions in general, but with his wife, he was more anxiously attached. My friend was indeed surprised by his own results, and he sent me this text along with his score:

> Hey there—I was shocked at my result which was secure—'cause I would say that's true but with Mia I am so 1000% no boundaries codependent so how could I get a secure attachment?

How can this person score as generally secure but anxious with his wife? Circle the correct statement.

1. This person has a personality disorder and hence is inconsistent in his emotions with different people.

2. This person's attachment style is all over the map. He must have made a mistake when filling out the questionnaire and needs to redo it.

3. There's something specific about interactions with his wife that makes it hard for him to remain secure.

4. Because this person had an avoidant attachment with his father, he's developed an anxious attachment style with his wife.

The correct answer is 3.

A little background is helpful here. My friend actually took this test while his wife was in rehab. Despite being mostly secure, because of his wife's alcoholism, he became more anxious in the relationship, and rightly so. His wife would disappear for hours without warning, sometimes not even returning home for the entire night. She received DUIs and several times passed out and woke up to find that she had fallen and injured herself badly. Even the most secure person could experience ongoing activation of the attachment neurocircuitry given these circumstances and would shift toward an anxious attachment style.

This highlights how even secure attachment can be destabilized in the face of repeated relational unpredictability—something that underscores the adaptability, and vulnerability, of our attachment neurocircuitry.

Now that you're more familiar with your attachment topography and realize that in addition to your main style, you may have a repertoire of styles within you depending on whom you're interacting with, it's time to roll up your sleeves and tackle each insecure style specifically in the upcoming chapters. Although part 2 is divided into chapters on anxious, avoidant, and fearful avoidant styles, the strategies for becoming more secure are woven throughout. To get the full benefit, it's essential to read all the chapters, regardless of your own attachment style—each of them contains tools that we can all use.

# 6

# The Anxious Attachment Style: Living with Perceptual Superpowers

On the first day of the school year, Natalie noticed that her nine-year-old adopted daughter instantly clicked with a new classmate who had just transferred in. While chatting with the girl's mother, she learned that the girl was also adopted.

As she watched the two of them together, she suddenly froze. In a flash, she just knew: They were sisters!

"I was standing there, and the other girl's mom was talking to me, but I couldn't even hear her. All I could focus on was how alike they were. The way they walked, their small gestures, it was uncanny. I looked at their faces, and to me, they were identical. Not in every detail—my daughter has hazel eyes, the other girl's are blue. My daughter's hair is straight, the other's has a bit of a curl. But their features, their expressions . . . it was all the same."

Overcome with emotion, Natalie shared her hunch with others. But they dismissed it. She told the teacher, her caseworker, and the other girl's mother, yet no one took it seriously. The girl's mother insisted she'd been told her daughter was the only child of the woman who gave her up for adoption. "People wanted me to let it go," she recalled. "But I couldn't. I couldn't deny what was right in front of me." Refusing to give up, Natalie began investigating on her own, digging through her records and trying to learn more about the biological mother and her background. After months of persistence, a caseworker finally agreed to look into it.

Eventually, the call came. "Are you sitting down?" the caseworker asked. "I have some news. You were right—the girls are sisters." Tears welled up in Natalie's eyes. "I'm so glad I didn't give up. It felt like a little miracle. Now my daughter gets to share her life journey with her sister."

Years have passed since that first day of school—and the two girls are still inseparable.

Natalie's story may seem extraordinary, but when you examine attachment research, you'll discover that it's not unusual for people with anxious attachment to see things that others often miss.

A functional MRI study by Zahra Nasiriavanaki and colleagues at Harvard found that people with anxious attachment showed heightened activity in brain regions that track approaching faces. They demonstrated that anxious attachers noticed approaching faces when others' brains didn't register a thing. At the University of Illinois, R. Chris Fraley and his team showed that anxious attachers pressed a button earlier than others when a face gradually shifted from neutral to emotional (sad, angry, or happy). This positioned them to see subtle changes in mood that others failed to notice.

And it's not only faces and expressions. People with anxious attachment also pick up on other signals in their environment. Tsachi Ein-Dor and Mario Mikulincer at Reichman University demonstrated that anxious attachers were the first to detect and report smoke seeping from a computer. In a related experiment, Ein-Dor and Orgad Tal found that when participants were instructed to deliver news of a malware threat, anxious attachers were more likely to persist in getting the warning to IT, even when another person deliberately tried to stall them.

These studies paint a clear picture: People with an anxious attachment

## THE ANXIOUS ATTACHMENT STYLE

style have a finely tuned nervous system that picks up on social and environmental shifts faster—and responds more strongly. These perceptual gifts can be incredibly useful in all areas of life. They can offer a major advantage in business and negotiations, lead to scientific breakthroughs, and help people become better caregivers or homeowners, to name a few.

The question then arises, where do these perceptual powers of anxiously attached people come from? The answer may challenge much of what we think we know about anxious attachment.

## THE ORIGIN OF ANXIOUS ATTACHMENT

Much of the research hypothesizes that anxious attachment starts in childhood—that it's the result of caregivers who didn't meet your emotional needs, leaving you less able to soothe yourself or feel safe in relationships. The assumption is that your parents didn't make you feel safe enough and as a result, you developed a kind of social hypervigilance—a built-in radar system that's always scanning for danger. But these ideas haven't been fully proven. In fact, the reverse may be true: People with anxious attachment may simply have exceptional senses that allow them to identify things others just can't. This does mean that as an anxious attacher you're good at picking up on hints of danger. But it goes well beyond that. It's not just danger that you are better at spotting. You can detect a whole world of nuance and subtlety that others often miss—just as Natalie recognized the resemblance between the two girls when no one else did.

Indeed, when you examine the research outside of those common assumptions and biases and focus solely on the data, a clear pattern emerges: Anxious attachers—about 20 percent of the population—possess remarkable perceptual abilities that far surpass those of others.

Viewing anxious attachment through the lens of perception superpowers rather than as a deficit in self-soothing also changes how we might think about their childhoods. Instead of seeing anxious attachment purely as a result of insufficient parenting, we might consider how incredibly demanding it could have been for parents to raise a child with heightened perceptual sensitivity. So the "poor parenting" that researchers observe and hypothesize as the cause of anxious attachment may simply reflect the real-world challenges that come with tending to a highly attuned child. Indeed, a whole body of research suggests that some of these enhanced social and perceptual sensitivities may even be hereditary.

## Orchids and Dandelions

As a child psychiatrist, I'm always amazed by how some children take to therapy like fish to water. In their daily lives they may quarrel with their parents, struggle at school, and feel weighed down by difficulties. Yet the moment they step into the therapy room, it's as if they transform in the midst of a supportive, nonjudgmental environment. It feels as though a genetic calling is being awakened—as if something deep inside them is lying dormant, just waiting for the right conditions to open up to the world and blossom.

We draw together, write books, and invent entire imaginary worlds, and through this creative play I watch in awe as they improve, change, and excel. For me as a therapist, it is one of the most powerful experiences to witness. So when I came across the biological theory of orchids and dandelions, it immediately made sense.

Several studies demonstrate that a certain portion of the population has heightened sensitivity to their social surroundings due, in part, to a specific variant of the dopamine D4 receptor gene they carry. In harsh conditions, children with this sensitive gene variant often struggle—they may have difficulty with emotional regulation, act out, or fall behind in early developmental milestones. As they grow, these same individuals may be more likely to get into trouble or engage in risky behavior during adolescence. But in supportive environments, the pattern flips: Children and teens with this sensitivity gene often thrive, outperforming their less sensitive peers by leaps and bounds.

Researchers have likened these genetically sensitive individuals to *orchids*: delicate and harder to raise, but capable of blooming beautifully when given the right conditions. By contrast, those without this genetic sensitivity—who tend to do reasonably well even in less-than-ideal conditions—are like *dandelions*: resilient and adaptable, able to grow just about anywhere. Dandelions struggle a lot less than orchids in poor conditions, but they also don't flourish like orchids do when things are good.

In short, the presence of this genetic sensitivity doesn't inherently lead to poor outcomes. Instead, it amplifies environmental responsiveness. Anxious attachers, many of whom may fall into this orchidlike group, are not doomed by their heightened perception—they simply need the right conditions for their traits to become strengths.

## The Superhero Struggle

If you're biologically wired like an orchid, you need the right conditions to truly thrive. But many anxious attachers get stuck in environments—external and internal—that block their path to security.

In my practice I have learned to appreciate how the exquisitely fine-tuned senses that come with anxious attachment play out in my patients' lives, with the specific benefits and challenges they bring.

These perceptual abilities can be remarkable. But, like superheroes in movies, powers left unchecked can get their owners into trouble. One of my patients described this double-edged sword in our very first session:

> I love interacting with people. When things click, I feel genuinely happy—it energizes me and helps me get things done. It's my happy place, and when I'm in that zone, I accomplish a lot,

and people love being around me. I'm really good at what I do—I find that I can identify trends in the stock market way before others do—and when I am confident enough to act on it, my firm reaps huge rewards.

But even though I'm very successful at work and am married with two lovely kids, things aren't as good as they seem on paper. I'm extremely sensitive to potential slights in relationships. I get hurt quickly—and when I do, it really affects me.

It might be a friend who snubbed me, a work colleague trying to undermine me, or my kids or wife giving me the cold shoulder. Whatever the situation, it ends up taking so much space in my mind I don't know how to let it go. When things get really bad I don't always handle it well. I sometimes lash out at the person involved and feel awful soon after. I then need to talk about what happened with someone else—just to get it off my chest. But I can go on and on about the same thing, which I know can wear people out.

And the worst part? Once I get activated like that, it doesn't go away easily. I don't have an off switch. The mental preoccupation can last a long time—anywhere from a few hours to several days. In more severe cases it can go on for weeks, even months.

I hate it.

I find this to be such an insightful description of the superhero anxious attachment struggle. When things go well interpersonally, you can excel and thrive, but if something is amiss, your keen senses can make it extra hard to let it go and get back on track. The same qualities that help you thrive—the heightened perception that Natalie showed and the conviction not to stop paying attention to it—then become your Achilles' heel. So how can you find peace with this perceptual superpower that can upend your world?

The solution is simple: If you create a secure environment for yourself, you'll be able to devote your sensory superpowers to positive life endeavors, and in turn you'll excel and flourish.

How do you create this kind of secure environment? That's where CARRP comes in.

CARRP, as a reminder, stands for *consistent, available, responsive, reliable,* and *predictable*. Think of it as the anxious person's superhero suit and armor, the secret weapon that keeps your heightened senses from turning against you. When people are CARRP with you, your radar no longer locks on to interpersonal strife. Instead, you can use your powers for the greater good, benefiting both yourself and those around you. Non-CARRP behaviors, on the other hand, are your kryptonite. They will weaken you and deplete your powers. A CARRP intervention, as outlined in chapter 2, is how you prime others toward the security you need to flourish. The more your daily exchanges, including the seemingly insignificant minor interactions (SIMIs) described in chapter 3, are CARRP, the more secure your world becomes.

When the vast majority of your SIMIs are CARRP, your perceptual strengths can be channeled into creating and thriving rather than being consumed by constant vigilance.

And though the solution is simple in principle, in practice, you'll have to overcome specific obstacles along the way.

## THE OBSTACLES THAT KEEP ANXIOUS ATTACHERS FROM BECOMING SECURE

What keeps so many anxious attachers from realizing their full potential?

In my experience, it usually comes down to two powerful obstacles, which I have come to call *attachment gaslighting* and *the protest-regret cycle*.

- *Attachment gaslighting* refers to the internal and external messages that make you doubt your perceptions.
- *The protest-regret cycle* is a painful attachment loop that keeps your nervous system locked in perpetual distress.

These two forces drain a lot of brain energy and leave you preoccupied and unhappy, just like my patient from the previous section. They reinforce insecurity, which stands in the way of creating the enriched social environment that you need in order to become more secure.

Let's look at each more closely.

## Attachment Gaslighting

I often caution my anxiously attached patients against attachment gaslighting: when you make yourself—or someone else makes you—feel like something is wrong with you simply because of your heightened perceptual abilities.

For instance, a friend might say, "You're reading way too much into this," after you notice they've been giving you the cold shoulder for several weeks—dismissing it outright. Or you may tell yourself, "I'm overreacting. I should just be able to go with the flow. They're just busy. Stop making a mountain out of a molehill." This can leave you feeling like you're too sensitive or that you're blowing things out of proportion.

Both the external and internal denials of your perceptions can then lead to enormous self-doubt. You end up struggling against your biology, trying to "tough it out" as others might, only to find yourself overwhelmed again and again. This cycle leaves you feeling ashamed, defective, or that you're "too much for others to handle."

What's happening isn't a flaw in you—it's the clash between non-CARRP SIMIs and your biology. There are many ways attachment gaslighting shows up—both internal and external.

# THE ANXIOUS ATTACHMENT STYLE

**INTERNAL GASLIGHTING:** When you are hard on yourself, you might think...

- "I'll be able to handle it."

  You put yourself in insecure situations and relationships thinking you'll be able to handle things and everything will be fine. You think, "Other people can; why can't I?" But denying your enhanced perceptual abilities is like putting an orchid out in the snow and expecting it to thrive.

- "I shouldn't let this get to me."

  Once you're in a non-CARRP dynamic, you berate yourself for being so affected. Instead of recognizing your reaction as valid, you judge yourself for having it.

- "It's because of my childhood."

  You justify putting up with present-day insecurity by pointing to experiences you had growing up. You tell yourself, "I'm only reacting like this because of my childhood—it's not because of this person's behavior in the here and now." But if a current situation echoes past wounds, isn't that even more of a reason to resolve it with a CARRP intervention or try to get out of it and instead surround yourself with secure experiences that can override those old patterns?

**EXTERNAL GASLIGHTING:** When others dismiss you, they might say...

- "You're too sensitive."

  People delegitimize your way of experiencing the world by making an overly broad judgment of you.

- "No one else would be upset about this."

People can invalidate your orchid biology by comparing you to the roughly 80 percent of the population whose nervous system functions differently than yours.

- "It's all in your head."

  This is actually true—it *is* "in your head" because your nervous system is picking up on things 80 percent of the population doesn't pick up on. But that's not how they mean it. They say it in a dismissive, almost mocking way—as if your perception isn't real or valid. But research I referred to earlier in this chapter shows that, in fact, it often is. These comments dismiss your experience and cause you to question your perceptions, even when these perceptions are accurate.

A friend of mine recently reflected on a dating-gone-awry situation. As things were getting more serious, she asked her partner to check in with her during the day—even just a cute emoji so they could stay connected. He responded: "You really expect me to text you in the middle of the day? We both have jobs. Don't you think that's excessive? I can't give you that—no one can. You're responsible for your own well-being, not me."

My friend felt flustered during the day when he didn't respond to even her occasional texts, and ultimately she decided to end the relationship.

At the time, she felt ashamed and convinced she was the one in the wrong, that she was simply too needy—despite my ongoing reassurance that she wasn't. "It takes two seconds to send a cute emoji," I reminded her. "It's not such a huge ask."

Months after the breakup, while we were walking together through Central Park, she said: "You know, I found out that he had multiple affairs at work. Can you believe it? I sensed something back then, and now I see he pulled a double whammy—attachment gaslighting and the good old-fashioned kind. My attachment system knew he wasn't really engaged. It infuriates me to think that, at the time, he managed to convince me that I was the problem. It's scary to think I bought into it."

## The Protest-Regret Cycle

If attachment gaslighting makes you doubt your sensitivity, the protest-regret cycle traps you in it. It's the second major obstacle that stands in the way of the anxiously attached becoming secure—and it is equally painful. At the heart of this vicious cycle, two key attachment mechanisms become triggered: protest behavior and activating strategies.

**PROTEST BEHAVIOR:** We all have a brain mechanism that monitors the availability of others. If you sense that the other person (whether a friend, coworker, or significant other) is unavailable or disengaged, this mechanism sounds the alarm. Your senses pick up on their distance and you feel a great sense of unrest until you reestablish contact. When you're successful, all's well again; but if not, you remain in a state of unease. Depending on the situation, you may even feel compelled to act in some way—for instance, by sending a simple text like "Everything ok?" or even just "?"; or by resorting to more extreme measures, like calling the person dozens of times or barging in on them. All is in the service of reestablishing that emotional tether (even if it means making them mad—for the attachment system, negative attention is often better than no attention). These attempts to restore a connection are called protest behavior.

**ACTIVATING STRATEGIES:** Another common reaction when we feel we've lost that attachment tether is activating strategies. These are internal responses generated by your attachment neurocircuitry—ingenious strategies your brain uses to keep you engaged in the relationship when you sense the other person has pulled away. An activating strategy can take many forms. It can be a thought, a feeling, or urges that keep the connection front and center. Activating strategies can fester for long periods of time in the anxious attacher's mind, taking up energy and space. It's one of the greatest sources of suffering and distress. You might replay conversations, stew in anger, fantasize about a reunion, experience feelings of guilt and regret, or just find it hard to think of anything else. Unlike protest behaviors, which are aimed at getting the other person to reengage, activating strategies are those thoughts and feelings that ensure *you* don't let go. They keep the relationship active, and all-consuming, in your mind. Even after protest behaviors die down, and even if they were not acted upon, activating strategies can linger, sometimes even for years.

Now that you know more about protest behavior and activating strategies, let's turn our attention back to the protest-regret cycle.

The protest-regret cycle happens when recurrent non-CARRP situations are built into a relationship. Because of your heightened perception, you have an uncanny ability to detect these attachment indiscretions, and they'll bother you—even if you wish they didn't. This creates a predictable pattern that repeats itself over and over, which is why I've come to call it the protest-regret cycle. I divide it into five stages.

## THE FIVE STAGES OF THE PROTEST-REGRET CYCLE

**STAGE 1: ACTIVATION OF THE ATTACHMENT SYSTEM.** You're getting along with the person, things are going well, and then a non-CARRP moment erupts. They pull away, ignore a message, or act cold or off. If you have an anxious attachment style, you pick up on it instantly. Your attachment system sounds the alarm, and you go into a state of rapid activation.

**STAGE 2: THE ONSLAUGHT OF PROTEST BEHAVIOR/ACTIVATING STRATEGIES KICK IN.** At first, you might try a soft protest, which is the emotional equivalent of knocking on someone's door. You call or text repeatedly, write emails, check their social media for clues, or replay recent conversations to figure out what went wrong. If that doesn't work, the protest escalates and may lead to a *protest blowout*—now you're in an emotional state that's akin to banging on their door, wanting to kick it down. When in that state, you might lash out, say something sharp or cutting, or go to the other extreme, giving them the silent treatment (stillfacing them), threatening to leave, or withdrawing completely, both physically and emotionally.

**STAGE 3: AN ATTACHMENT BACKLASH.** After you calm down, a strange thing happens. You experience an *attachment backlash*. You feel that your response was too extreme and have enormous guilt and regret about how you behaved. You miss the person terribly and worry that you hurt them with your words and behavior. With the same intensity you had when you blamed them for what happened, you now blame yourself. Activating strategies lead you to engage in fierce internal attachment gaslighting—"It's all my fault, I made a mountain out of a molehill, I said all these hurtful things"—with no end in sight.

When activating strategies surge, they often flood anxious attachers with longing, guilt, and self-reproach, pushing them to reengage—even when part of them still remembers the pain of being hurt. These strategies rarely let up until you give in and reach out, doing their bidding.

**STAGE 4: RECONCILIATION AND RESIDUAL RESENTMENT.** Because, as an anxious attacher, you have a sticky attachment system that doesn't let go of other people easily, you find yourself feeling terrible remorse about the relationship rupture. You seek reconciliation and end up apologizing. But as you apologize, you sense a foreshadowing of regret for the apology, too—there's some resurfacing resentment because the original non-CARRP behavior was never properly addressed or resolved. The focus shifted to you and your "terrible" behavior rather than what caused it. But you cut your losses and resume closeness anyway, knowing that if you don't, it will be too painful.

**STAGE 5: AN ADDITIONAL NON-CARRP INCIDENT.** Inevitably, another non-CARRP incident emerges, starting the cycle all over. Sometimes you try to endure your upset and keep it bottled up—attempting to be the dandelion you never were. But your keen orchid senses remain hyper-engaged, and your nervous system builds up activation pressure until an even bigger blowout happens in response to what may seem like a minor incident. This leaves the other person confused about why a small infraction deserves such a "disproportionate" reaction, making you seem even more unreasonable or, worse, "unstable," when, in truth, it's a response to tension that's been accumulating over time. This lands you right back at the beginning, and you find yourself going through the protest-regret cycle once more. To emphasize the potential cost of the protest-regret cycle in your life, I've included a flowchart on the next page.

## COLLATERAL DAMAGE: THE PROTEST-REGRET CYCLE AND THE BURNING OF SOCIAL BRIDGES

Another outcome of the protest-regret cycle is that, when you're in protest mode, you instinctively seek solace from others to help you deal with a painfully upsetting situation. Just like the patient I described earlier in this chapter, you can't stop talking about it with your trusted confidants. You recount the awfulness of the other person but often share an extreme, one-sided version of events—leaving out any redeeming details that might offer nuance or context. In doing so, you're not rallying people to "your side"—you're actually rallying them to your *insecure* side.

Then, when the attachment pendulum swings back and regret sets in, you realize you went too far in villainizing the other person. Now you're left trying to mend the rift—while your support network, who heard only the extreme version, is criticizing you for doing so. This leads to addi-

## THE ANXIOUS ATTACHMENT STYLE

**A Life of CARRP versus Non-CARRP for the Anxious: Living Securely with Perceptual Superpowers***

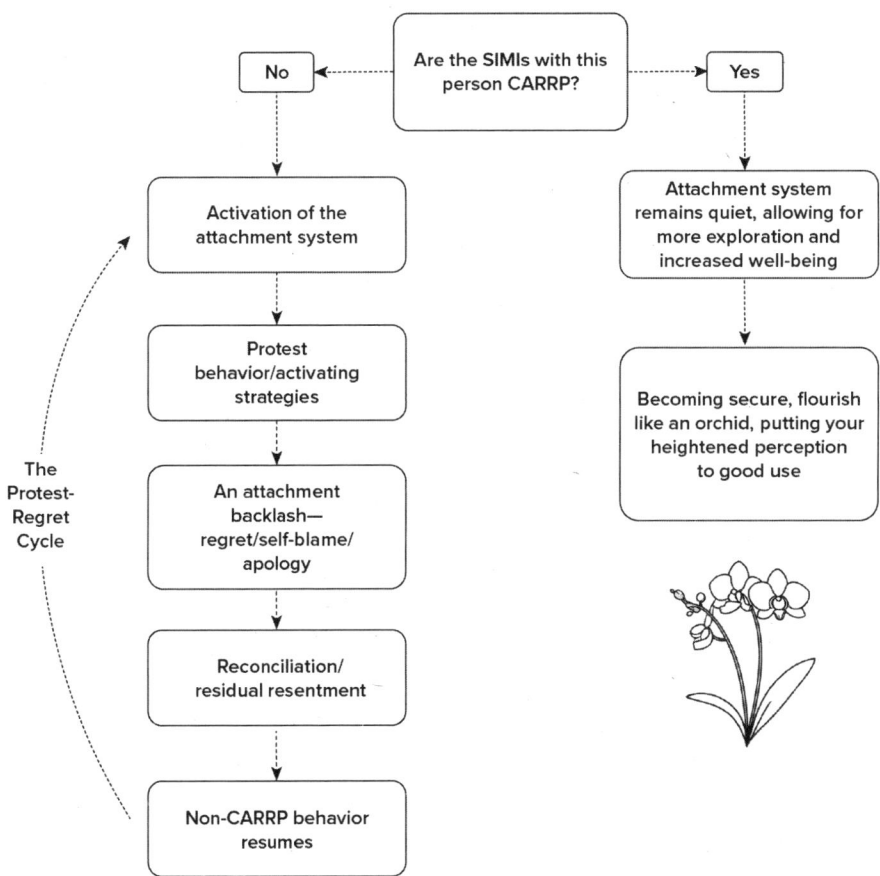

tional stress and insecurity with your go-to people, which interferes with the secure goal of forming a hyperconnected life (see chapter 2).

The best way to avoid this scenario is to include the other person's perspective when you share; how *they* might see the situation. For example,

---

*CARRP = Consistent, Available, Responsive, Reliable, and Predictable
SIMIs = Seemingly Insignificant Minor Interactions (of everyday life)

let's say a work colleague you usually collaborate well with snubs you by leaving you out of a project. You feel hurt and go around telling others how awful the person is. But later, you remember how well you typically work together and realize you may have misjudged things. Now you're stuck. How can you go back to collaborating after tearing them down with your coworkers?

When you're upset and turn to others for comfort, try to offer a more secure, balanced narrative of events, one that invites perspective, not just your protest. For example, you might say, "I'm really upset right now, and I know I'm presenting a one-sided view. If I try to see it from their side, they might say that I am not knowledgeable in this area and that's why they didn't ask me."

It's also important to go to your *secure allies* for help. The ones who help you stay grounded. They'll say things like "So they didn't include you this time, but you know how much they value you. Is it possible that it's not deliberate? You two usually collaborate so well and produce amazing work together. It's not worth throwing all that away."

This kind of support helps you de-escalate and return to a more balanced, secure view without burning your support bridges (more on that in chapter 13 on Secure Coaching). Notice that they didn't discount how you feel. They didn't engage in attachment gaslighting by saying you're overreacting. Instead, they primed you by reminding you of some good aspects of the relationship.

When you're less upset, keeping a balanced view will help you weigh the situation more carefully. But remember, you do have unique senses, and this is not an invitation to engage in attachment gaslighting. Instead, when the attachment system quiets down, you can proceed with a CARRP intervention, if necessary, and evaluate the quality of the collaboration moving forward (see more about collaborative assessment in chapter 11).

## CREATING A SECURE SCRIPT TO RIDE THE PROTEST-ACTIVATION WAVE

If you find yourself wanting to engage in the protest part of the protest-regret cycle, it can be helpful to pause and follow this script in order to see the situation from a more grounded, secure stance.

Ask yourself:

- What would a secure person do?
- What might be their point of view on this issue?
- Have I ever acted in a similar way toward someone else?
- Will I regret saying or doing something right now?
- Is it possible I don't need to say or do anything at all, and that I can just sit tight and wait?

You can think of your script as a way to avoid saying or doing something inflammatory that could set the protest-regret cycle in motion or make it worse. Instead, the goal is to ride the activation wave until it passes and you're calm enough to deal with the situation more securely.

Secure people are good at handling conflict because they respond from a less activated place. You can do that, too, once you've learned to ride the wave and wait until you're settled before responding. It might take time to calm down, and your attachment system will try to convince you it's urgent to act now, but don't fall for it.

You have a lot to lose by jumping into protest-regret mode and everything to gain by staying grounded, riding it out, and coming back to the situation later, when your system is back to baseline. Remember, you picked up on something that needs to be evaluated. Don't discount your senses. But it is the feeling of *urgency*, of needing to *act now*, that is often misleading and can work against you.

## ANXIOUS BURNT-OUT MODE

Once the protest-regret cycle repeats itself several times, you know better than to rock the boat too much—it's just too painful and nothing gets resolved. You learn to live within the confines of an insecure relationship, but you never really get used to it. Rather, you become apathetic, with some flare-ups here and there. And it comes at a price—you are continuing an interaction that is detrimental to your nervous system and that is keeping you from becoming secure.

Anxious burnt-out mode can even get to the point where you feel like you've become avoidant because you stop caring. But the numbness of anxious burnt-out mode isn't avoidance. It lacks the empowered avoidant mindset of "I can conquer the world on my own." Instead, you just shut down and withdraw. You don't desensitize and move on—you retreat into yourself, quietly surrendering, learning to survive in emotional lockdown.

So how do you break free from this protest-regret cycle and the anxious burnt-out mode that stand in the way of your achieving security? How do you create an environment that lets your super-perceptive abilities shine? Fortunately, there's a way—and it's more straightforward than you think. You have to learn to apply the *Appendix Rule* when performing CARRP interventions.

## THE APPENDIX RULE: YOUR EXIT STRATEGY

I call this take-no-prisoners approach to CARRP interventions for the anxiously attached the Appendix Rule because of an old surgical custom where surgeons would remove a noninflamed appendix in at least 10 to 20 percent of cases because the alternative could be horrific. Underdiagnosing and missing appendicitis is a real danger; an inflamed appendix can burst and the infection can spread to the whole abdomen, leading to hor-

# THE ANXIOUS ATTACHMENT STYLE

rible illness and long-term complications. This is why doctors were taught to be overzealous in ruling in favor of surgery, even if it meant removing a healthy appendix.

The same principle applies to your nervous system. Non-CARRP relationships can be viewed as inflamed social appendices that threaten the well-being of your nervous system. You want to aggressively issue non-CARRP verdicts in your CARRP interventions, even at the price of downsizing relationships that you cherish, to avoid letting insecure SIMIs fester in your life. This doesn't mean that you have to cut people out of your life; the secure approach tends to be much more temperate. Believe it or not, simply trying to cut ties with someone—even if they hurt you or wronged you—can activate your attachment neurocircuitry and lead to an attachment backlash.

The Appendix Rule states that as soon as you recognize a non-CARRP pattern in a relationship, you must disengage and deprioritize it. No ifs, ands, or buts. If you take a look at the flowchart presented on page 109 about the radical difference between a CARRP and a non-CARRP relationship for the anxiously attached, it will immediately become apparent why. The difference between having a life in which you thrive and a life in which you engage in an endless activation loop is just so stark. To see how this plays out in real life, let's look at Marsha's story.

### Marsha's Story: The Appendix Rule in Action

When Marsha moved to a new town, she quickly bonded with her neighbor Lorna. They shared a love of theater, literature, and the arts, and their conversations flowed easily. But over time, Marsha noticed something that unsettled her. Lorna rarely shared things—where she got her hair cut, her favorite shops, or even a doctor's name when Marsha was searching for one. For Marsha, who delighted in sharing good finds and referrals with friends, this felt strangely withholding—and painful.

She tried to bring it up gently, mentioning that as someone new in town, it would mean a lot to get help with those things. But nothing changed. Each time Lorna withheld something, Marsha would feel stung and pull away, only to then later drift back into their previous routine, caught in a cycle of hurt and upset.

In therapy, Marsha began to understand that this wasn't just about a few missing recommendations. She had a deep-seated need—and a genuine talent—for closeness. Her heightened perception made her exquisitely aware of even subtle forms of disconnect. What she thought was her own "overreacting" was actually a form of internal gaslighting, denying her accurate perceptions and need for CARRP SIMIs. That meant she had to be more intentional about whom she let into her inner circle.

So she applied the Appendix Rule. She didn't cut Lorna off. They still exchange warm hellos and occasional chitchat when they run into each other. But Marsha gently moved Lorna to the outer circle of her life and instead poured more energy into people like her new friend Jackie—open, generous, and fully CARRP. The contrast was profound. With Jackie, there were none of the insecure moments she experienced with Lorna. Instead, she felt connected and genuinely cared for.

For someone with an anxious attachment style, this kind of intentional shift—building a CARRP inner circle and gently repositioning others—can mean the difference between anxious burnt-out mode and a life where closeness becomes a nourishing force that helps you truly flourish.

Notice that Marsha didn't cut ties with Lorna altogether; instead, she just lowered the volume on that relationship. The way Marsha did it is of the utmost importance in successfully applying the Appendix Rule. As an anxious attacher, you will have a hard time letting go of close relationships, even when they're harming you. In Secure Therapy, Marsha learned to use a crucial tool to help her do that, a tool that you, too, will need to master—Wall Tennis with Love.

THE ANXIOUS ATTACHMENT STYLE

## WALL TENNIS WITH LOVE: LETTING INSECURITY FADE INTO THE BACKGROUND

How do you lower the volume on an insecure relationship without setting off your attachment neurocircuitry? To avoid the emotional roller coaster of the protest-regret cycle, you need to do it gently, in a way that will keep your attachment system from getting activated.

If you've ever tried to play tennis against a wall, you know that it's relatively easy—what you serve, the wall will return right back to you. The wall won't surprise you in any way. It won't initiate a stronger serve or send you running in the other direction. Rather, the wall will return the ball in your direction with a slightly lower velocity.

When it comes to dialing down non-CARRP relationships, you essentially have to become the wall. You don't initiate interactions, you don't make the tie stronger or weaker—you just reciprocate with kindness and love, while slowly letting the other person recede into the background of your life. This way, you also leave room for them to come back in the future—maybe circumstances have changed, maybe they are more secure and the SIMIs with them aren't so draining. But for now, you play Wall Tennis with Love while simultaneously immersing yourself in secure SIMIs with people who are CARRP.

This is what Marsha did with her friend Lorna. When Lorna texted, Marsha always responded. She was kind and warm. When invited to do things, she'd usually decline, but occasionally she'd join Lorna if it didn't mean spending too much time together; for instance, they'd take a quick walk with the dogs or have lunch with other friends. If Lorna brought something up, she responded with warmth. She remained the wall, responding with kindness to anything that Lorna sent her way but in no way initiating or trying to maintain the relationship spark.

## THE UPSIDE OF AN ANXIOUS ACTIVATED STATE

Up till now we've talked about an activated attachment state as a source of unhappiness and suffering for anxiously attached people. But an activated attachment has an important function. In crucial moments, being activated helps summon all your strength to let you focus on assisting the people you love. This happened to my friend Muriel.

When Muriel heard that her mother was diagnosed with breast cancer, she was scared. Her mother was in her early sixties, had always been health-conscious, and seemed resilient and well. Now, suddenly, chemo, surgery, and radiation were looming. Muriel immediately sprang into action; she packed a suitcase and flew to New York. On her way there, she kept texting her mom: "How are you doing?" "Is everything okay?" "Do you need anything?" Her mom replied, "Yes, still fine, I'm okay," with smiley emojis. Muriel couldn't think about anything but her mom. She reached out to her friends and contacts to find out who would be the best doctors in New York. On the plane, she fought back tears and couldn't stop thinking about what might happen to her mom. She was anxious in the cab from the airport but experienced a sense of relief when she walked through the door to find her mom looking like her normal self and smiling at her. Muriel hugged her for several minutes, not wanting to let go. The physical closeness quieted her attachment system.

Activation of the attachment system isn't always triggered by someone being unavailable, failing to meet your needs, or engaging in non-CARRP behavior. It can also happen when a loved one needs help. In these moments, the same forces that make you obsess about the person who wasn't available become your asset. You hunker down and become hyperfocused on the person who needs you. In Muriel's case, her anxious, activated state became a strength. During the course of the treatment she picked up on subtle shifts in her mom's expressions, alerted the medical team early, and pushed for better care. The same energy that might have gone into ruminating about a friend who didn't call—checking their social media feed, replaying the last conversation—was now fully focused on helping her mom. She couldn't leave her bedside. She was consumed with her care, and nothing else mattered.

## THE FINAL STEP—FREEING YOUR BIOLOGY

As an anxious attacher you have both the need and the *ability* for a lot of closeness. This understanding is paramount for your well-being.

In prehistoric times, it was advantageous to have people in the population who were intensely drawn to closeness. They loved affiliating and interacting with other folks, and this may have helped advance the human intellectual revolution through increasingly sophisticated social networks. Secures can get along in any situation, but for anxious attachers, being close with others is paramount for their health and well-being, and given the right conditions, they may outperform everyone else.

Ironically, the same human progress propelled by close human collaboration gave rise to a modern lifestyle marked by less connection and more isolation, where, thanks to technological advancements, people often live alone, are far from family, work remotely, and spend more time on screens than with others.

An illuminating global study led by Tyler VanderWeele and colleagues at Harvard's Human Flourishing Program surveyed more than 200,000 people across twenty-two countries and uncovered a striking, counterintuitive finding: People in some lower-middle-income nations—such as Indonesia, the Philippines, Nigeria, Kenya, and Tanzania—reported higher levels of overall flourishing than those in many wealthy countries, including the U.S., the UK, Japan, and Germany. Flourishing was measured using a six-domain index that assessed happiness, health, meaning and purpose, character and virtue, close social relationships, and financial and material stability. Each domain included two questions. For example, participants were asked whether they felt their lives were worthwhile (meaning) and whether they acted to promote good even under difficult circumstances (character). Despite lower economic development, many participants in the lower-middle-income countries reported stronger communal bonds, a clearer sense of purpose, and more consistent moral engagement—factors that appear to support well-being even more than technology or wealth. These findings challenge the assumption that progress and prosperity automatically lead to better lives, highlighting instead the powerful role of communal engagement.

I believe that these findings have special relevance for people with anxious attachment style, whose need for love and closeness makes them especially vulnerable to the lack of strong human connection and social bonds.

Here's where the importance of an enriched social environment, discussed in chapter 3, comes back into play. Anxious attachers, who are frequently focused on protesting the unavailability of one specific person, often just need a quick reminder of their special affinity for closeness to help them go out into the world and engage with others to create an enriched social life for themselves. Increasing their social engagement leads to a dramatic shift in their well-being, moving their attachment dial to greater security and contentment.

This was the case for David. David would always get upset with his girlfriend, Jill, for not paying him enough attention, instead spending time with her friends or working late. He constantly felt slighted by her busy schedule, and as a result, he'd use protest behavior with a vengeance: He'd stillface her, roll his eyes when she spoke, and speak unkindly to her. She would get upset and sleep on the couch. Things would only escalate from there, and eventually she'd bring out her suitcase and start packing, threatening to leave.

In treatment, I worked with David on how to communicate his hurts more effectively and resort less often to protest behavior, but we went beyond that. David and I discussed that putting all his focus on Jill wasn't working for him. He had both the need and the ability to be close to many people, and trying to fulfill that need with a single person simply wasn't enough. This led to frequent quarrels and upsets, a pattern that had repeated itself in several of his prior relationships as well.

David set out to prioritize his social circle. He rekindled friendships from his childhood, from high school, and from college, and he made an effort to make new friends. He joined a weekly meditation group as well as an acting improv class and made sure to be in touch with his parents several times a week. It wasn't hard for him to implement these changes—he liked being social. But spending time with friends and family had just fallen by the wayside with his sole focus on Jill.

Before long, David had a busy social life to keep his need for closeness in check. He is now so immersed in this rich world that he hardly ever experiences perceived insults from Jill. I used to tell him that he needed to be in a car full of people to be happy. We now jokingly say that he needs not a carful but a busload, and that's perfectly fine!

## FINAL THOUGHTS FOR THE ANXIOUS ATTACHER

Throughout this chapter, I've shown you that anxious attachment is not a deficit or problem to be fixed but a unique set of perceptual superpowers that—when properly channeled—can be a tremendous asset to you and the people around you. Like any superpower, anxious attachment comes with both responsibilities and challenges. My aim in this chapter has been to help you harness these gifts in your quest to become more secure.

# THE ANXIOUS ATTACHMENT WORKSHOP

## Tom's "Okay" Struggle

Tom began to feel sick at work. It hit fast—one minute he was fine, and the next he had chills, body aches, and a pounding headache. By the time he got home, he was congested, exhausted, and running a fever. When he tested himself, he discovered he had the flu. Tom shot a quick email to his boss, letting her know. His boss replied quickly with a simple "Okay." Tom was flabbergasted. He stared at the email in a state of disbelief. "Is that it?" he asked his husband. "No 'Get well soon,' 'Keep us posted on how you're feeling,' 'Rest up and feel better'? Nothing more than a single word?" Tom agonized over the email the whole week he was at home sick. It was almost worse than the flu itself. His husband told him he was making too much of it. "She was just super busy. Don't read so much into it," he said. "You're blowing it out of proportion and making yourself miserable for nothing. You always do this."

Which of the following is/are correct?

1. Tom's response is a perfect example of an activated attachment system.
2. Tom should have done a CARRP intervention and sent another email to his boss letting her know that he was offended she didn't wish him a quick recovery.
3. Tom's perception of the situation should not be underestimated.
4. Tom's partner was right; he was reading too much into it.

The correct answers are 1 and 3. As someone who has an anxious attachment style, Tom's heightened sense for non-CARRP behaviors should not be underestimated. He can pick up on small cues during his interactions with his boss, and his reaction to this one was likely a culmination of many insecure SIMIs with her that he could probably recall if probed more carefully

Three weeks after he returned to the office, Tom was let go. He'd had a hunch this was on the horizon. His boss often didn't give him credit for his work and funneled some of the projects he initiated to others. Over the three years they'd worked together, there was always tension between them, and he was never part of her inner circle. He knew something about his boss's reaction to his email wasn't right. It triggered a sense of danger, and he was correct in his assessment. He came home and told his husband, who was shocked, even though Tom wasn't surprised at all. Still, Tom agonized about being let go.

Which of the following are ways his partner can help him?

1. By highlighting that in Tom's case, rejection is protection.
2. By telling Tom he will do much better in a secure workplace, and his boss was anything but secure.
3. By realizing that while some can fare okay in an insecure workplace, it is crucial for Tom to have a supportive environment.
4. By telling Tom to move on and not fixate on his old job. It's getting in the way of his search.
5. By letting Tom know that, though it might bother him for a while, eventually he will let it go and be happier.

All answers were correct but number 4. Tom is like an orchid: He does exceedingly well in supportive, nurturing environments and quite poorly in insecure surroundings. He will be better off finding another workplace where he can feel more secure. While others might weather his boss's curtness, Tom is bothered by it to no end. In his case, rejection is truly a form of protection, because he now gets a chance to change his environment. But telling him to move on isn't helpful. Tom would gladly do so if he knew how to. It's much harder for an anxious person to turn off their radar and let go. Over time, it's possible to do, but for now, instead of telling Tom to stop thinking about it, offering some distractions may be much more helpful—going to a ball game, watching a movie, or more specifically addressing the issue by finding ways to help him in his job search.

## ANXIOUS ATTACHMENT CHEAT SHEET

To create a secure, hyperconnected environment:

1. Be consistent, available, responsive, reliable, and predictable (CARRP).
2. Determine if other people around you are CARRP.
3. Perform CARRP interventions.
4. Assertively assess relationships using the Appendix Rule.
5. Use Wall Tennis with Love to deprioritize non-CARRP connections.
6. Create an enriched social environment.

# 7

# The Avoidant Attachment Style: Living Comfortably with a Measure of Distance

One of my patients, Brian, once described his experience with his avoidant attachment style to me:

> I interact with people, and then at some point I just need some space for myself, and I shut them out of my awareness. Most of the time I'm not even fully conscious that I'm doing it; I just find myself busy and immersed in work and other things, and I don't think about them much. It's not that I don't mean to call or text, or that I don't want to be in touch; I just don't really think about it. Then, when I get angry texts or emails that I'm thoughtless and selfish, or if I do reach out and get snubbed, it always catches me by surprise. I don't understand what I did wrong, and I feel bad that I upset them, but then I also get resentful that I now find myself in this all-too-familiar position again of having to apologize and make an extra effort to "be better" when all I really did was mind my own business, living life on life's terms. It only reinforces my feelings that nothing I do is

ever good enough, that people are too needy, and that I can't trust or rely on others because they will turn on me and get upset with me. I can only rely on myself.

If you have an avoidant attachment style, you may often find yourself inadvertently triggering other people's attachment alarm systems, leading to painful and unhappy insecure interactions. Unbeknownst to you, you create the very SIMIs that run counter to what you need in a relationship in order feel more secure, which is space. But it doesn't have to be this way.

This chapter arms you with tools for overcoming common yet easily corrected avoidant pitfalls by creating secure SIMIs in your life. Secure SIMIs play a key role in giving you the freedom and space you need to form successful bonds. But before we dive into the tools, let's consider the basic biology behind the preference for distance or closeness and how it relates to the avoidant attachment style.

## THE NORWAY REINDEER—
## WHEN DISTANCE IS SAFER

In 2016, 323 reindeer were found dead in the Norway countryside from what appeared to be a freak accident. On a damp, cold, rainy day, lightning struck the herd as the reindeer were huddled together to stay warm. In a flash, they were all electrocuted. While this may sound like an unusual coincidence, there are several accounts of such occurrences. Guinness World Records notes that the largest number of cattle ever reported to be killed by a single lightning strike is 68. There are reports from China that 143 goats were killed in a lightning strike, too. And in 2021, 16 people died when lightning struck a wedding celebration in Bangladesh.

It turns out that there are risks to being close to others. The evolutionary outcome? In a great many species, some individuals possess gene variants that make them shy away from closeness. Just as some people are tall

## THE AVOIDANT ATTACHMENT STYLE

and others short, evolution ensured that some individuals would keep a measure of distance from the group so that, in the event of mass calamity, a portion of the population would be more likely to survive.

A vivid example of this principle can be found in *C. elegans*, a microscopic worm that is widely used in neuroscience research. When examined in the lab, *C. elegans* shows two distinct feeding behaviors—a social pattern and a solitary pattern. Most *C. elegans* feed in a mass frenzy. Once a few of them discover a source of food, the rest immediately join the party and form a huge pile of worms, all voraciously gorging. However, a small number of *C. elegans* were observed to eat in solitude. Under the microscope, you can see that when another *C. elegans* crawls in their direction, solitary *C. elegans* quickly crawl away. In fact, they maintain a safe distance at all times because they are chemically repelled by a substance the others secrete, whereas the social feeders are chemically attracted to one another. Astoundingly, this difference in behavior was found to be attributable to a difference in a single amino acid in a single gene—the NPR-1 (neuropeptide receptor 1) gene. In social feeders, there's one type of amino acid—phenylalanine—at one key spot in the protein. In solitary feeders, that same spot holds a different amino acid—valine. Remarkably, scientists have been able to switch *C. elegans* from social to solitary—and vice versa—by swapping these amino acids at that specific spot!

The tendency for individuals of the same species to show a mix of social and solitary behavior isn't limited to *C. elegans*—it's common across the animal kingdom. Some individuals are simply biologically wired to prefer being alone. Even individual pets differ in their preferences for closeness and distance. Some cats are "like dogs"—super affectionate and eager for closeness—while others will claw you if you try to pet them. Some dogs shy away from closeness—they'll stay loyal and protective but keep their distance rather than snuggling up. An innate preference for closeness and distance is all around us. All you need to do is observe and notice it for yourself.

And that, in a nutshell, perfectly captures what I believe is the experience of people with an avoidant attachment style: an unmistakable, biologically rooted preference for maintaining a certain measure of distance from others.

It's important to emphasize that there are advantages to having an avoidant attachment style beyond surviving a catastrophic event that wipes out an entire population. Research has shown that avoidants often function well under pressure at work, and are capable of making tough decisions on their own and executing them with precision. This may be due to their ability to "tune out" others more easily than people with other attachment styles. Additional research suggests that avoidants are less swayed by convention or what others think, often forming more individualistic points of view, a pattern mentioned to me by Geoff MacDonald, a prominent attachment researcher from the University of Toronto. In chapter 6, when we discussed the study where the researchers staged a potentially dangerous situation by having smoke pour out of a computer, I noted that anxious attachers were the first to identify the danger. What I didn't tell you is that once the anxious alerted everyone to the potential danger, it was the avoidants who were the first to flee, prompting others to follow.

## THE ORIGINS OF THE AVOIDANT ATTACHMENT STYLE

You will often hear in public discourse that avoidant attachment in adults results from distant, deficient parenting. The idea is that the child, learning that they cannot rely on the parent, develops a coping mechanism where they forgo, or even actively suppress, their need for the closeness that has been so scarcely available to them. In other words, they learn to fend for themselves. Over the years I have observed, both in my practice and in people around me, that this isn't necessarily the case. Some people

## THE AVOIDANT ATTACHMENT STYLE

with an avoidant attachment style had warm and loving upbringings. This was the case with Julia.

Julia came from a religious background. The youngest of six, she was always lavished with attention and affection. However, growing up, she noticed that her friends had a different outlook on life than she did. While they were all thinking about getting married and having kids, Julia couldn't even fathom that idea. Whenever someone she was dating mentioned the words *commitment* or *marriage*, she'd run for the hills. There was nothing to suggest that her lack of interest in closeness and commitment stemmed from a cold, inattentive upbringing; on the contrary, she was loved by all, siblings and parents alike. Still, she felt her best when she was independent and self-reliant.

In our Secure Therapy sessions, we identified Julia's need for a measure of distance from people and discussed the idea that when she met potential partners, she could start by relating that—she would tell them she needed a slower pace and a lot of space.

Soon thereafter, she met Matt. Matt wasn't threatened by her need for space and gave her plenty of it. As a result, she didn't feel the urge to run away. Eventually, it was she who uttered the word *marriage* to him, and he wholeheartedly agreed. There wasn't any healing from childhood events that she needed to get through to reach a place where she could feel close. She just needed a brand of closeness that suited her to be able to feel secure in a relationship, and Matt was able to give her that.

If you have an avoidant attachment style, you just don't feel comfortable with too much closeness; it makes you squirm, and you feel suffocated. People who don't have this need for distance often make you feel that something is wrong with you, that this need for space is the result of a troubled upbringing and should be fixed. But what if you're avoidant not because of trauma resulting from distant parenting that, if healed, would lead to a greater desire for closeness? What if, instead, you're simply wired to like your distance, and no amount of "healing" would change that? In that case, you might be doomed to an internal struggle and potential frustration that you're "not getting better," when, in reality, you'd be better off finding a way to live in peace with this basic trait. In fact, as was the case with Julia, when avoidants get the distance they crave, they feel much better and can be quite happy and content.

So how do you go about gaining that safe distance while simultaneously nurturing strong, happy relationships?

I will suggest an approach that circumvents this question of where avoidance came from altogether. It will help you feel more comfortable in relationships so that you can slowly grow accustomed to being close without feeling suffocated, regardless of your attachment history. The solution is simple: You must make peace with the closeness-distance paradox, and you must learn to be CARRP.

## THE CLOSENESS-DISTANCE PARADOX

To understand the closeness-distance paradox, you first need to consider the following important assertions in attachment science:

- From the point of view of the social brain, relationships exist to make you feel safe.
- You typically feel safe, and your nervous system is calmer and more settled, when you and others around you are CARRP.
- When you feel safe, you engage in an exploration of the world around you.

It's easy to see how these assertions play out, and what happens when these conditions fail to exist, when you observe toddlers and little kids.

If you bring a toddler into a room full of toys, right away they start pointing at everything in the room with delight, immediately interested in exploring their surroundings and playing with the exciting newfound

## THE AVOIDANT ATTACHMENT STYLE

treasures. As long as the toddler knows that their caregiver is available if they need them—and they do look back and check to see if their caregiver is nearby from time to time—they engage in exploration and play and don't care much about anything else. But the minute they feel their caregiver is not available—for instance, if the caregiver leaves the room—they lose interest in the toys, rush to the door calling for their caregiver, and begin to sob. If the caregiver is delayed in coming back, they will cry harder, sometimes even falling to the floor and thrashing about, demanding their caregiver's presence.

As an avoidant, when you feel you need your own space and abruptly withdraw from people, you act like the caregiver who leaves the room and triggers the attachment neurocircuitry in their child. You are inadvertently creating a situation in which the other person is now perceiving potential danger, and as a result, they seek more closeness, more engagement, more contact, when all you really wanted was a little downtime to yourself. In other words, by abruptly withdrawing—leaving the metaphorical room—you activate the other person's attachment neurocircuitry and trigger their protest behavior. Which is exactly what Brian so eloquently described as happening to him in all of his relationships, much to his bewilderment and upset.

And this, in essence, is the closeness-distance paradox: A secure connection leads to independence and exploration, and an abrupt withdrawal from that connection leads to an immediate shutdown of exploration and a frantic hyperfocus on the person who withdrew.

In other words, a little closeness can lead to a lot of distance.

The solution is simple: Make sure not to trigger the alarm systems of the people you're close to, and they won't bother you much. They'll be too busy exploring.

How do you achieve that? By being CARRP, and it's much easier than you think.

## CARRP: THE AVOIDANT'S TICKET TO A STRESS-FREE LIFE

Being consistent, available, responsive, reliable, and predictable may be the furthest thing from your mind when you just need a little time away. But you're in luck. CARRP is the ultimate relationship pacifier. The attachment neurocircuitry that oversees the closeness-distance paradox doesn't require much in the way of hand-holding. You just need to proactively calm the system before it blows up. A well-timed response, sent *before* the other person starts to worry, will usually do the trick with minimal effort.

I'm always amazed by how well this works. Avoidants usually stage an uphill battle with other people's attachment neurocircuitry. But by keeping a measure of consistent availability—that is, by staying in touch for a minute or two through a quick text or call—you help others' attachment systems stay dormant. Instead of triggering protest behavior, you align yourself with their attachment neurocircuitry, keep it calm, and—voilà—you get the peace of mind and space you crave.

Even though being CARRP is straightforward—just give a little attention here and there to the people in your life—for you, the avoidant, it may be difficult to master initially because it asks you to override your instinct to stay self-sufficient and your belief that each party is responsible for their own well-being. But with some work on your part, you can master the art of CARRP. And once you do, it will pay off by leaps and bounds.

Shirin experienced the effects of implementing CARRP in her life firsthand. She had a very anxious teammate, Miles, who would email and call many times a day—especially when they were working on a high-stakes project with a tight deadline, which was exactly when Shirin most needed her space.

Shirin habitually ignored Miles's emails and calls until she had finished her work; at the end of the day, she would respond. However, when she finally did get on the phone with him, the conversations were tense and unpleasant. Miles would often complain that she was not responding to his calls. Once, as they were pushing toward a particularly stressful deadline, he got so angry that he yelled over the phone, "I just can't deal with you anymore. You make me so mad I want to bang my head against the wall!" Shirin ignored his complaints. She wasn't there to manage his anxiety; she was there to get the job done.

After learning about CARRP, Shirin changed her strategy. When they were working on a high-stakes deadline, she would send a preemptive email each morning to let Miles know that she was hard at work and wouldn't be able to talk before 4:00 p.m.—but that she'd send a quick update around lunchtime. At noon, she'd follow up with a short note reporting her progress and reiterating that she was looking forward to connecting later in the day. She also let him know that if there was an important question or something urgent, he should reach out, but she'd prefer that they discuss everything on their afternoon call. When 4:00 p.m. rolled around and they got on a call, the conversation was calm and productive. Miles was much more at ease—even happy with their collaboration.

The beauty of learning how the attachment neurocircuitry works is that, once you understand its quirks, you realize that it doesn't require much from you. Miles didn't want to talk on the phone for hours while they were busy, wasting both of their time. He just needed to connect briefly during the day to keep his attachment neurocircuitry at bay.

For Shirin, ignoring Miles's calls and emails was like being a parent who leaves the room only to come back hours later, having let their child cry themselves to distraction. When you do that and activate the other person's attachment neurocircuitry consistently, the consequences can be quite devastating.

## THE THREE PITFALLS THAT STAND IN THE WAY OF AN AVOIDANT BECOMING CARRP

On the road to becoming more secure, avoidants face specific hurdles. Recognizing them will help you stay on course.

### Pitfall One: You Go It Alone; Why Can't They?

One of the basic tenets of attachment science is that when something bad happens to you, you'll reach out to your attachment figure for help and support. They are your safe haven. As an avoidant, you find it hard to be that person. But it's not your fault. Let me explain.

When something bad happens to you, instead of being motivated to reach out to others for help, your avoidant wiring pushes you to deactivate, meaning your impulse is to minimize the need to reach out to anyone. So you hunker down and try to get through things on your own. This makes helping others who come to you for reassurance when they are distressed quite challenging. As they approach you, you find yourself taken aback. You don't fully understand why they are looking outside themselves for support. Why can't they handle their own feelings? Why are they so needy?

This makes you take a few steps back. Surprised and hurt that you aren't helping, the other person, who is already in a compromised emotional state, begins to protest. For them, the original reason they reached out seems insignificant now compared to the pain caused by your withdrawal. Unknowingly, you added insult to injury, and you end up the focus of their distress. This becomes suffocating and unbearable for you, making you shut down even further. Your basic programming and instincts cry out, "What do you want from me? Heal thyself!"

If you can come to terms with the fact that your avoidant reaction is the odd one out and that, unlike you, most people need emotional reassurance in times of need, and you can learn to give others that reassurance,

# THE AVOIDANT ATTACHMENT STYLE

you will save yourself a lot of agony and keep yourself from becoming the subject of their intense attention when you fail to come to their aid.

## Pitfall Two: Messing with Attachment Homeostasis

"I did all this for you, and you still want more?"

"Nothing I do is ever good enough."

"I wish I had never even tried."

I often hear these statements from avoidants in response to upsets from people in their lives. Such statements stem from one major issue: a lack of understanding of what attachment homeostasis is about.

As an avoidant, you may unknowingly find yourself instinctively engaging and disengaging with closeness. It's just how your attachment style is wired. I'd watch out for that. Let me explain why.

When you're in good spirits, you feel close, let loose, and enjoy quality time with your partner, friends, or family. Then you've had enough—in fact, you've gotten more than your fair share of closeness and need some downtime. The problem is, when you go all in on closeness and then disappear, the other person gets activated and starts to protest. And their protest behavior really gets on your nerves—understandably. You showed up and connected in a big way, which doesn't come naturally for you—and even that isn't enough?

You don't realize that what you've done is mess with attachment homeostasis, which is a fancy biological word for stability. You disrupted the stability of the relationship, and this makes the other person super sensitive to any potential distancing. They can become quite *needy*, another word for protest behavior. You unwittingly bring about this predicament with your own behavior.

Steph and Rich had an amazing weekend together. They started with a play followed by dinner at a Michelin-star restaurant where they enjoyed the chef's tasting menu. The next day, they went shopping and Rich treated her to a designer purse. On Monday, he was busy and forgot to text her in the morning and around lunchtime the way he usually did. When he called her that evening, Steph was cold and distant. The following night, he was too tired to have sex—for the first time ever. That's when Steph broke down and said she was sure it was over, that he had changed his mind and wasn't interested in her anymore. "It's always this way; people get close and then they change their minds and leave," she told him. "I can tell when it's happening, and I can tell it's happening with you."

Rich got angry. "How can you think that after the amazing weekend we just spent together?" he said in a harsh tone. "Are you even listening to yourself?" He was clearly upset and said he wasn't going to discuss it any further. But Steph couldn't fall asleep. In fact, his anger and the fact that he hadn't reassured her provided further proof, in her mind, that he was "over her." The next evening, Rich let her know by phone that he was busy the rest of the week and could only see her on the weekend. Steph told him that she knew what he was doing—he was pulling away. She hung up abruptly, and Rich was livid. "There's just no end to her neediness," he thought to himself. "I'm not sure this is going to work."

Not understanding the importance of attachment homeostasis and the CARRP SIMIs that are needed to maintain it is a recipe for relationship strife that isn't exclusive to romantic bonds. It occurs with friends, with family members, and even at work when you give someone a lot of attention and then pull back. The relationship upsets that result from these disruptions can easily be prevented by making sure you don't abruptly withdraw or change your baseline. And if you happen to anyway, instead of getting upset with the person when they protest, the way Rich did, provide them with the reassurance that they need. It's all well and good to have an amazing weekend together and let yourself embrace closeness, even to go above and beyond with grand gestures of expensive gifts and meals, but be aware that you can't then just disappear without suffering the attachment repercussions. Be prepared to offer a bridge to your usual distant self by providing lots of reassurance for as long as necessary. After all, the person is not upset with you—which is always the thing that gets the avoidant angry. They're activated because of a disruption in the delicate attachment equilibrium that now needs to find a new calm.

The avoidant vicious cycle and its antidote become clearer when laid out visually. The flowchart on the next page shows a life of CARRP versus a life of non-CARRP for the avoidant. Not being CARRP sets off the cycle of protest, forced closeness, and escalating tension. But when you are CARRP, you keep the attachment neurocircuitry calm, others shift their attention outward into the world, and you get the space you need while moving toward greater security.

## Pitfall Three: Closeness Overdose—Biting Off More Than You Can Chew

For you, the avoidant, it's also important not to heap too much closeness on yourself all at once. You need your distance, so baby steps are the way to go. This can be counterintuitive. When you finally feel comfortable enough to be close, shouldn't you go all in? Or sometimes, after a bout of closeness, when the urge to retreat kicks in, you might try extra hard to push through it, to prove that you can stay connected. The problem is, you may bite off more than you can chew—which is exactly what happened to Sheila.

Sheila and Jeff's relationship had a tumultuous start. They were each involved with someone else when they met but found themselves irresistibly drawn to each other. Sheila had an avoidant attachment style and was often unresponsive and unpredictable with Jeff, but also with her kids and at work. She would say she was going out for a quick walk but wouldn't come back for hours, or she'd say she'd call at a certain time only to call the next day. Jeff asked her to be more CARRP, but she found herself struggling to grasp the concept and how to apply it. Nevertheless, initially things were amazing between them. They both expressed that they

## A Life of CARRP versus Non-CARRP for the Avoidant: Living Securely with an Inherent Need for Distance*

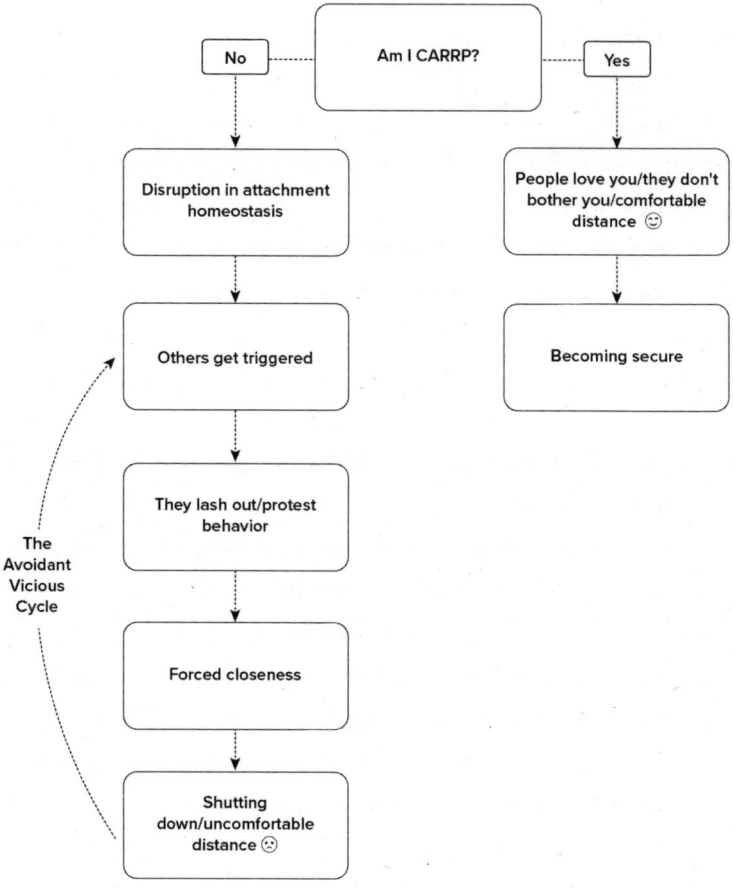

connected sexually, emotionally, intellectually, and spiritually, more deeply than they had ever connected with anyone else.

At some point, Sheila began to feel suffocated, which scared her. She didn't want to lose that special feeling with Jeff, so instead of withdrawing—her natural instinct—she decided to double down on her efforts to forge closeness with him.

---

*CARRP = Consistent, Available, Responsive, Reliable, and Predictable

The following week, Jeff had minor surgery. Sheila made a point to stay with him in the hospital the entire time. A few days later, it was his birthday, and she insisted on organizing a party and personally inviting all his friends. But very quickly it became overwhelming for her and backfired. She ended up abandoning the party early and proceeded to disappear for a few days, not answering calls or texts. Despite her best intentions, she couldn't muster the strength to follow through with her plan to push herself to stay close.

Sheila started to think that maybe this relationship wasn't right for her and question whether she'd made a mistake in leaving her previous partner for Jeff in the first place. In attachment science, these kinds of withdrawal responses are called *deactivating strategies*—thoughts and actions, like pulling away, ghosting, or convincing yourself the relationship is wrong, that allow avoidants to dampen the intensity of closeness when it feels overwhelming. Jeff was devastated by the way Sheila had ghosted him. He didn't ask her, nor did he particularly need her, to spend all that time with him in the hospital or organize his birthday party. He was perfectly fine without those things. But her disappearance was just too much for him and hurt him terribly, and when she came back several days later, he broke up with her. Sheila felt an enormous sense of loss over the breakup, and the original urge she'd had to flee the relationship, which stemmed from deactivating strategies because of too much closeness, was all but gone. Instead, activating strategies—the ones that drive you to seek closeness—came rushing in, and she felt alone and ashamed.

People with an avoidant attachment style who don't understand or appreciate the importance of CARRP in driving secure SIMIs often find themselves trying too hard—doing all the wrong things to compensate for their need for space. They try to establish closeness with grand gestures, but then these backfire, leading avoidants to become overwhelmed and disappear. This, in turn, creates an even starker difference and leads to greater activation and hurt in the other person.

The solution? Pace yourself by sticking to SIMIs that are CARRP and avoiding the grand gestures. Start small and build on that. It will allow you to ease into closeness with others much more comfortably.

## AN OUNCE OF PREVENTION IS WORTH A POUND OF CURE

A few final words, for you, the avoidant attacher: The goal of this chapter has been to familiarize you with the quirks of your attachment style and teach you specific tools to work with your biology rather than against it. When you learn to do that, you begin to move toward security, gaining greater satisfaction and peace of mind in your relationships.

For the avoidant person, being CARRP means first admitting to yourself that you have a need for space, and then getting comfortable explaining that need. The sooner you let people know, the better, and it's not enough to do it only once or twice. It's important to keep the conversation going throughout all your relationships in a way that will convince those around you that it's about your general need for more space for yourself and not directed at pushing them away. On the contrary, you want them in your life, but you have to strike the right balance that lets you show up for them. The more you can do that, and the more people you can surround yourself with who can securely accept it, the better off you'll be. Those who can't tolerate the kind of distance you need will find others who are more like-minded.

At the same time, your need for distance doesn't mean that you are exempt from doing your part. In this chapter, I have taught you how to be CARRP and walked you through the potential pitfalls that might get in the way of that. My hope is that, over time, you will become more skilled at being CARRP and in doing so avoid some of the traps you tend to fall into that activate and hurt those around you. The goal is that you'll feel comfortable enough to build stable CARRP relationships with a wider circle of people, helping you become more secure.

I used to say that when it comes to attachment needs, you want to extinguish a small flame before it becomes a forest fire, but now I'll take it a step further and say that you want to try to make sure no one's playing with matches at all.

## CARRP IN ACTION: A GUIDED EXERCISE FOR AVOIDANTS

Avoidants often rely on what attachment science calls deactivating strategies—automatic thoughts or actions that create distance when closeness feels too much—which is what Sheila did with Jeff. Many of these show up as non-CARRP behaviors. The good news is that each one has a simple CARRP alternative that can calm others' attachment neurocircuitry, ultimately leading you to get the space you need.

This exercise is designed to help you focus more specifically on habitual non-CARRP behaviors that you might engage in, so that you can come up with new CARRP ones instead. The more CARRP you become, the easier it will be to manage your relationships, the less constrained you'll feel by them, and the less likely you'll be to flee.

**Examples of non-CARRP behaviors and their CARRP alternatives:**

| NON-CARRP (DEACTIVATING STRATEGY) | CARRP ALTERNATIVE |
|---|---|
| Ghosting or disappearing without explanation. | Let the other person know you need downtime, while reassuring them of your commitment. |
| Saying "I'll call you right back" but not following through. | If you can't call, send a quick text to acknowledge that and then set realistic timing for when you can talk. |
| Acting warm and close, then suddenly going cold. | Keep your tone and responses steady, even if brief. |

SECURE

| NON-CARRP (DEACTIVATING STRATEGY) | CARRP ALTERNATIVE |
|---|---|
| Ignoring texts or emails until the other person is frantic. | Send a short acknowledgment ("Got your message, busy now, will reply later"). |
| Withholding personal details or feelings. | Share small, genuine bits of yourself so others feel included. |
| Remaining emotionally distant, refusing to open up. | Offer a brief emotional truth ("Rough day, a bit stressed") to signal presence. |
| Refusing to ask for help, insisting on self-reliance. | Allow yourself to ask for small favors or reassurance—it builds trust without loss of independence. |
| Not offering to help others, assuming they should manage alone, and disappearing in their time of need. | Extend small gestures ("Want me to pick that up?" / "I can listen if you need") to show availability. |
| Walking several steps ahead or behind instead of side by side. | Slow down and walk together—even without conversation, physical closeness reassures. |
| Withdrawing physical affection (avoiding hugs, leaning away). | Allow brief, predictable contact (a hand squeeze, a short hug) to keep connection alive. |
| Skipping events that matter to the other person. | If you need to bow out, acknowledge the importance of the event and express interest afterward ("Tell me how it went"). |
| Leaving abruptly when overwhelmed. | Signal your need for space gently ("I need a little time alone, but I'll be back later, text or call if you need me"). |

# THE AVOIDANT ATTACHMENT STYLE

Now, write a few scenarios from your own life.

Example:

**Your habitual non-CARRP behavior:**

When I feel overwhelmed after spending a lot of time with Milly, I sometimes ignore her messages. That makes her frantic, which frustrates me and pushes me to withdraw even further.

**The CARRP behavior you could use instead:**

I should explain openly that I need some alone time and find a way to do it that doesn't hurt her, while reassuring her of my commitment. I need to remain CARRP in the relationship, which will make Milly focus less on my actions and whereabouts and give both of us peace of mind.

It's your turn:

**Your habitual non-CARRP behavior:**

_____

_____

_____

**The CARRP behavior you could use instead:**

_____

_____

_____

SECURE

**Your habitual non-CARRP behavior:**

_____

_____

_____


**The CARRP behavior you could use instead:**

_____

_____

_____

8

# The Fearful Avoidant: Taking a Leap of Faith into Closeness

I often think of the fearful avoidant attachment style as locking yourself away in a tall fortress tower to protect yourself from getting hurt, yet still yearning for closeness. It's a self-imposed Rapunzel setup, if you will, except without the long locks of hair to pull anyone in.

This approach to self-protection is adopted for good reason. People with a fearful avoidant attachment style find relationships to be extremely challenging. Having high relationship anxiety and, at the same time, high relationship avoidance often leads to painful, confusing, and unhappy relationship interactions. You may love with all your heart and have the best of intentions, yet time and again you find it difficult to make closeness work.

In the previous two chapters, we covered tools that those with anxious and avoidant attachment styles can use as they strive for greater security. For you, the fearful avoidant who possesses traits from both attachment styles, it's especially important to read those chapters first. They will give you tools to address your anxiety and avoidance, while here you'll get the opportunity to integrate those approaches and expand on them. We'll also unpack some of the unique challenges that you might face so that you, too, can take strides toward a secure life.

## COME CLOSER! STEP BACK! THE FEARFUL AVOIDANT CYCLE

Abe constantly complained that his fiancée was working long hours at the office and that he wanted more closeness and time together, but when they were together, things didn't always go well. If he felt his fiancée made even the smallest mistake—booking the "wrong" restaurant for date night, for example—he would become livid inside, overwhelmed with negative thoughts about how incompetent she was. "What kind of a mother will she be to my children," he'd fume, "if she can't even do something as simple as find a good place for dinner?" He even went so far as to contemplate breaking up with her over this. On the other hand, when they were at home together, he often felt that his fiancée was being distant. If she was reading a book instead of watching TV with him, he would experience it as a personal affront and give her the silent treatment. Meanwhile, she kept wondering what she might have done wrong. These hot/cold behaviors and his frequent ups and downs made the relationship extremely unstable.

If you are a fearful avoidant, you yearn for closeness and reject it at the same time. It's as if with one hand you are signaling "Come closer" but with the other signaling "Stay away." Your avoidant side, which insists on maintaining a safe distance, runs at odds with your anxious side, which longs for closeness and is sensitive to the threat of distancing. The result: an endless loop of insecurity. When you feel too close, you deactivate—you use specific thoughts and actions that create distance between you and your partner. But once you gain that distance, your anxious part activates, triggering thoughts and behaviors that attempt to draw your partner closer. These usually take the form of protest behavior, which can be destructive to the relationship. This was the case for Abe: When he felt too much closeness with his fiancée, he would find fault with little things she did—a classic deactivation strategy. Then, when she was not close enough, he would punish her with silence to provoke a reaction—a common protest behavior.

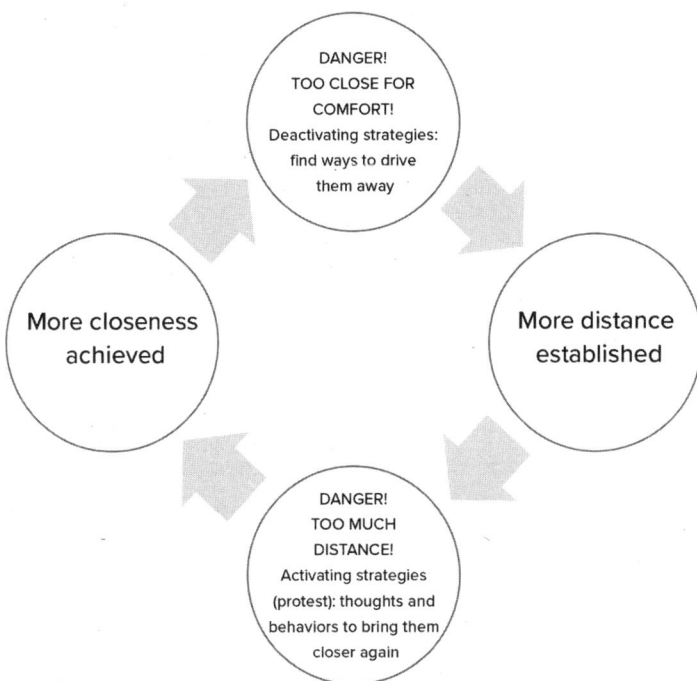

The Fearful Avoidant Inner Trap

The result of this endless loop: Either you swear off relationships altogether because you don't want to fall into this vicious cycle or, when you do form a close relationship, you find yourself in a tumult that leaves very little room for new CARRP SIMIs that can help move you toward security.

Many postulate that the fearful avoidant attachment style stems from past traumatic relationships, in which closeness went hand in hand with threatening and abusive behavior, leading to both a yearning for and a rejection of close connection. I believe this to be the case, but regardless of whether this cause and effect is indeed true for you, in this chapter we will work on helping you progress toward greater security and healing.

How do you start on that path? By building a secure base that will slowly, with baby steps, ease you into relationships that don't make you want to bolt on the one hand or make you feel the connection is in constant jeopardy on the other. By cautiously creating an environment where you feel comfortable and safe, you will jump-start the healing process in your brain.

## BUILDING A SECURE VILLAGE: INSTRUCTIONS FOR FEARFUL AVOIDANTS

For you more than for anyone else, it's of the utmost importance to give primacy to secure SIMIs in your life. This means surrounding yourself with people who are CARRP and exercising the Appendix Rule, which entails actively weeding out insecure interactions. But even when your life is full of secure interactions, your work isn't done. You also have to learn to pace them so that you yourself can remain CARRP and not feel trapped by too much closeness. Letting too much closeness in too quickly can send you running for the hills, perpetuating relationship instability.

Providing the fearful avoidant brain with secure SIMIs is like nurturing a tiny bird hatchling found in the wild. You have to feed the hatchling just the right amount—initially only tiny morsels of food regularly and frequently. Too much will make the bird sick; too little and it will starve and fail to grow. To nourish your security, you need to expose yourself to a steady, carefully paced stream of secure SIMIs. These will, in time, create a safe social surrounding that allows your secure self to grow stronger and more resilient so that it can fend for itself and leave the nest.

Tammy had a history of tumultuous relationships. Growing up, there was always yelling and emotional upheaval in the home. Her father was

## THE FEARFUL AVOIDANT

abusive, and he isolated Tammy from kids her age, locking her up in her room and insisting that she needed to study. For most of her childhood, she was completely alone. Yet despite this, because of her enormous grit and high intelligence, Tammy flourished as an adult. She went to graduate school and became a thriving professional.

When she came to see me, Tammy had just been through a painful breakup. Though she seemed to have many friends, when she described the various dynamics of her close relationships, it became clear that she had no close, secure relationships. One "friend" would often get drunk and then lay into her, insulting her about her life and her "flawed character." Another was kind to her but utterly unreliable. She would cancel plans on a whim. Once, they were supposed to go to the Catskills for the weekend only for the friend to cancel in a text when Tammy was already in the rental car on her way to pick her up.

Tammy's family was no better. On every call, her parents made derogatory comments, and she would often find out after the fact that her siblings had had a get-together without her. These interactions devastated Tammy, and we would discuss them at length in treatment. Tammy was clearly fearful avoidant. Despite yearning for closeness, she was afraid of letting new people in and was exquisitely sensitive to perceived slights from her social surroundings. At the same time, when people were CARRP and wanted closeness, she would reject them or at best keep them at arm's length.

In our Secure Therapy sessions, we began to work on building Tammy's secure base. She used the Appendix Rule to lower the volume on her non-CARRP friends and family, and over the course of the first year she interacted with them less and less. She didn't cut things off entirely; instead, she employed Wall Tennis with Love, which we discussed in chapter 6, and it worked. These insecure relationships slowly faded into the background of her life.

Bit by bit, Tammy began to nourish secure SIMIs with people both at work and in her personal life. She became selective about work projects, declining to take on certain commitments when she suspected that the people she would be working with would engage in insecure SIMIs. She took on only projects where she felt the SIMIs would be primarily secure. This meant she lost some business initially, but her schedule quickly filled up with more secure opportunities.

In her personal life, Tammy rekindled friendships with secure friends from high school and college. Some lived in different cities, which suited Tammy, because they could visit each other on occasion but the geographical distance allowed her not to feel suffocated or burdened by too much closeness. What's more, as a long-distance friend, expectations of her were different, and that suited her just fine. She didn't have to attend social obligations that she didn't care for, and time differences with some of her friends meant there was a smaller window where she had to be available for calls. She even conducted some friendships mostly through text. They rarely spoke on the phone, and it felt just right.

The thing that really changed Tammy's life was Scruffy, the rescue mutt she adopted from a dog shelter. Scruffy turned out to be the most secure influence in Tammy's life. His cuteness and helplessness disarmed her, and his ferocious, unwavering, secure love was a breath of fresh air. Tammy decided to leave the bustling energy of the city and moved to a country home on Long Island, where she and Scruffy would go on hikes in nature. This also helped her form connections with people in her new town, as most everyone stopped to chat and comment on how cute Scruffy was. Tammy eased into spending her days in her quiet, sun-filled living room with Scruffy, reading and working.

Over time, Tammy developed a carefully paced, secure social life in which she found peace. However, when it came to dating, she continued to struggle. On online dating apps, she swiped left on everyone; she wouldn't give anyone a chance. They all seemed wrong for her. If someone had a nice body, they seemed conceited; if they were even slightly out of shape, that was a problem, too. If she did go on a date and the guy texted her soon afterward, that wasn't good, either—even if she liked him—

because she'd feel cornered and suffocated. But as her sense of security grew, she began to take small leaps of faith and give people a chance.

Eventually she met Marc, who was able to give her the safety and security that she needed. He was utterly CARRP, some might say even to the point where he was quite rigid about schedules, and honest to a fault. He did have his own quirks. For example, he once threw a fit because she kept the showerhead turned sideways and not exactly ninety degrees to the wall. He was particular about these kinds of details, and he shared that he was on the autism spectrum. This might have been challenging for some, but Tammy found solace in his predictability and unequivocal candor. Tammy herself admitted that if it weren't for Scruffy, the secure village she'd built, and the resetting of her expectations and behaviors around relationships, she probably would not have been able to let Marc in.

### STEPS TO BUILDING A SECURE VILLAGE FOR THE FEARFUL AVOIDANT

1. Make sure the people in your life are CARRP.
2. Immerse yourself in secure SIMIs.
3. Very important: Make sure your exposure to closeness is gradual. Don't overdo it! Slow and steady wins the race.
4. Remain CARRP. By being CARRP, you ensure you don't bring insecurity into your life. (See "CARRP in Action: A Guided Exercise for Avoidants" in the previous chapter.)
5. Use CARRP interventions on non-CARRP people.
6. If non-CARRP interactions persist, apply the Appendix Rule. You really want to weed out these interactions to cement a secure change.
7. Use Wall Tennis with Love to lower the volume on insecure connections. Gradually deprioritize insecure relationships in your life to promote healing.
8. Take a leap of faith by letting more secure people into your life over time.

## CARRP INTERVENTIONS FOR THE FEARFUL AVOIDANT STYLE

To build a secure village the way Tammy did will require you to engage in CARRP interventions. By intervening with yourself as well as with the people around you to maintain consistent, available, responsive, reliable, and predictable behaviors, you allow secure SIMIs to flourish in your life.

For someone who is singularly more anxious or more avoidant, striving for security is like being a rock climber carefully scaling a cliff using ropes, harnesses, and anchors to secure themselves so that they don't fall into an abyss. The anxiously attached have to find ways to subdue their fears and insecurity in their relationships, while the avoidantly attached have to avoid falling into the familiar pattern of pushing people away.

If you are a fearful avoidant, you need to take on an even more challenging task. Rather than being like a rock climber, who has to watch out "only" for one abyss, you are more like a tightrope walker with nothing to grab onto for safety. You must manage a delicate balancing act to keep from falling into the anxiety abyss on one side and the avoidant abyss on the other. You need to manage your tendency to get hurt when you perceive that others are pulling away, while at the same time managing your tendency to push them away to gain some distance. So when doing a CARRP intervention on yourself and others, it's important to understand that you need to walk a fine line between two opposing forces: anxiety and avoidance.

When Tammy first met Marc, she wanted him to text her more, but she also knew from experience that if he texted her too much, she would find it off-putting. So she performed the following CARRP intervention: She asked Marc to text her in the morning, midday while she was at work, and at night, but she emphasized that more than that might make her feel overwhelmed because of her busy schedule. He got it completely. Each day she received a "GM babe" text, a simple emoji at lunchtime, and a sleepy emoji at night. If she needed more on any given day, she would text and say, "Today I need a bit more encouragement and attention. Can you text me a few more times? I may not be able to answer, but it will be great to hear from you." The next day, if he texted more, she would say, "It was so helpful to get all your texts yesterday, but we can go back to our usual baseline now. I'm doing fine."

Performing CARRP interventions is especially challenging for fearful avoidants because they have to adjust to new secure behavior on two counts—learn to be less avoidant and less anxious while managing two opposing insecure forces pulling them in opposite directions. If this is you, it means you must navigate between your need for closeness and support, your fear of others letting you down, and your need for independence and space. By learning to respect your needs and desires in both the anxious and the avoidant dimensions—as Tammy did—rather than trying to ignore them, with time and practice, you will be able to execute CARRP interventions with grace and skill.

## STOPPING YOURSELF IN YOUR TRACKS AND APOLOGIZING: THE FEARFUL-AVOIDANT SECRET SECURE WEAPON

Brad was often beset with negative emotions and thoughts about his partner. Sometimes they were deactivating emotions or thoughts; for example, criticizing his partner in his head or at times to their face. He might tell his partner that they were not as good-looking, creative, or smart as they believed they were. Sometimes he would just get annoyed with how they ate or how they sneezed and say something snappy about it. Other times, his negative emotions were more activating in nature—he would feel extremely hurt by the smallest signs of distancing he perceived in his partner. For instance, he would get upset if they were studying in the same room and his partner didn't pay him any attention, or if his partner didn't call or text during the day. When that happened, he would either lash out or stillface them.

In treatment, Brad could see how these behaviors worked against the secure relationship he wanted to build. He was striving to become more secure, putting a lot of effort into it. He learned to be more aware of the negative emotions that engulfed him and not to act on them. Yet sometimes he found himself falling into old habits and saying or doing mean things to his partner. Then, in our Secure Therapy sessions, he learned how to do something that was a game changer for him. Rather than try to correct an insecure interaction by apologizing after the fact, he learned how to do so *while it was happening*. First he tried with all his might to avoid saying anything upsetting, but if he caught himself doing it, he learned to stop himself in his tracks and say: "I'm sorry for being unpleasant. I hate it when I'm like that. I'm saying things that I don't even mean because I'm upset, and I can't help it. I don't want to, though. Please help me get out of this headspace. I'm sorry."

When you have a fearful avoidant attachment style, it can get the better of you. Studies show that as a fearful avoidant, you tend to engage frequently in arguments and fights, and there's a lot of instability in your connections with others. You are overwhelmed by negative emotions and thoughts about people in your life, and these can come out even as you're working toward becoming more secure, setting you back. If this happens, do not despair. The key is to recognize that it is happening, stop yourself in your tracks, and apologize in the moment. When you do so, you essentially salvage an interaction that started out as insecure and divert it toward security.

Stopping Yourself in Your Tracks and Apologizing is a game changer because:

- *You stop the insecure behavior as it unfolds, minimizing relationship damage.*

- *You let your secure intentions shine through.* You convey that you don't want to hurt the other person and you're working on improving yourself.

- *You essentially learn to monitor your insecure behavior in real time.* The more you do it, the less often the unhinged, insecure behavior will occur, leading to greater security.

- *Where there is distance and strife, you create closeness.* Rather than increasing the distance, you create more closeness. By stopping yourself in your tracks and spelling out the situation to the other person, you include them in your struggle to become more secure—you show a vulnerability that inspires togetherness rather than a rift.

- *It helps to remind you of a key function of relationships*—to strengthen and regulate each other's emotions, not dysregulate them and make each other miserable.

- *You stop the vicious cycle of hurting and being hurt.*

## TAKING A LEAP OF FAITH: HOW TO MOVE FROM A FEAR-BASED LIFE TO SECURITY

Fearful avoidants are called this because they are terrified of closeness. While regular avoidants who dismiss their need for connection take pride in their independence, both anxious and fearful avoidants crave intimacy—with one big difference.

When anxious people meet someone they like, they tend to jump in headfirst, ignoring potential red flags and reservations. They dive into the pool, while fearful avoidants don't even dare approach the edge of it, paralyzed by the fear of getting hurt. When you are a fearful avoidant, anything that signals the potential for closeness makes you scream, "Stay away, don't take a chance, don't go there!" despite your deep-seated longing for closeness. And not without reason. People will fail you, and people will hurt you. But letting fear rule your close relationships is like throwing the baby out with the bathwater. People will also love you and protect you and change you in the most profound and wonderful ways imaginable.

To ease into it, you can start with safe bets, such as joining groups where closeness is less threatening. For example, try a running group, theater class, meditation course, or exercise program where you meet and talk to people but there are no high school–style cliques or drama, and you feel a comfortable sense of togetherness. You can then choose a few ultra-secure people from your enriched social milieu and invest your time and effort in them. They will teach you the ways of a secure life.

But in each attempt to get close to someone, you have to take a leap of faith. The goal of this chapter has been to give you tools to make that leap easier, but you still need to plug your nose, approach the edge of the pool, and jump.

# 9

# Test-Drive Your Attachment Knowledge

In our daily lives, we encounter attachment dynamics everywhere we turn. But we don't often think about them from that perspective.

I find it helpful to assess relationship challenges from an attachment point of view. It gives each issue an extra layer of emotional depth and inspires different, surprising ways of approaching and solving relationship problems.

In this chapter, you'll get the chance to sharpen your attachment knowledge and skills by looking at everyday relationship scenarios. You'll be presented with a series of vignettes, each followed by a multiple-choice question. Think about how attachment might be at play, pick the answer that feels right to you, and then check out the discussion that follows. There, I'll walk you through the correct answer and explain why it makes the most sense.

And don't worry if you don't get them all right—the goal isn't perfection, it's practice. What matters most is learning to see the world through the unique prism of an attachment lens.

## MEAN AMANDA

Sixteen-year-old Suzie stopped talking to her friend Amanda because she was mean to her. Amanda constantly played hot and cold—sometimes she was sweet and friendly and then she would turn on Suzie, say unkind things, or ignore her at lunch. She would also go out with their mutual friends and purposefully exclude her. Now, three weeks after they stopped talking, Suzie finds that she misses Amanda terribly and can't stop thinking about her. She's confused and troubled by the fact that she misses someone who mistreated her so badly.

Circle the most correct statement.

1. Suzie is right to cut ties with someone like Amanda. Good riddance.
2. Suzie did the attachment equivalent of cutting off her nose to spite her face and is now experiencing the backlash of the protest regret cycle.
3. Suzie was too sensitive. There are tons of issues like that in girls' friendships, and she needs to learn to roll with the punches.
4. Instead of severing ties, Suzie should have given Amanda a taste of her own medicine—ignore her, make plans without her, and so on. It would have made Amanda grovel her way back.

In abruptly cutting ties with Amanda, Suzie resorted to a form of protest behavior. Even if in the moment she was confident this was the right decision, now that she's calmed down, she's facing an attachment backlash. If you're angry in the here and now and feel resolute in your decision to end a relationship, your attachment neurocircuitry may surprise you later in its intensity: This neurocircuitry literally causes changes in the brain that make certain people special and important to you in a powerful

## TEST-DRIVE YOUR ATTACHMENT KNOWLEDGE

way that's not so easy to undo. Even if you had valid reasons that justified severing the tie, when the attachment neurocircuitry gets triggered after you calm down, demanding a return to closeness, you find yourself longing for them. To avoid this pitfall, it's better to refrain from dramatic exits and let attachment sleeping dogs lie. You don't have to abruptly disconnect; you can just let a relationship fade into the background using Wall Tennis with Love (see chapter 6). This is especially important if you have an anxious attachment style, because anxious attachers don't have an easy kill-relationship switch. They can stay activated for a long time, remain preoccupied with the relationship for months, sometimes even years—and suffer a great deal as a result.

It's important to note that cutting ties is not really a decision you have much control over. The attachment system has a mind of its own and a rationale that overrides yours. Essentially, it operates from an evolutionary perspective, harking back to when humans were hunted animals in the middle of the food chain. At that time, it was better to have mean Amanda next to you than to have no one at all. If a lion charged, mean Amanda's presence still cut your chances of getting eaten in half, from a guaranteed 100 percent to 50 percent. The emotional part of your brain hasn't entirely caught up to the fact that you're no longer a hunted animal in the middle of the savanna and that you'll be okay without Amanda by your side; in fact, you might be better off that way. When you employ Wall Tennis with Love, you essentially pacify your attachment neurocircuitry, ensuring it remains calm while you quietly leave the relationship with no attachment backlash. The correct answer, therefore, is 2. Interestingly, 4 would have gotten Amanda's attention and might have reengaged her in the friendship, but it would have continued the insecure attachment pattern to Suzie's detriment. Answer 1 may be correct, but it just is so much harder to pull off when the attachment system is activated. Answer 3 is incorrect—we saw in chapter 1 how damaging and distressing the Cyberball effect can be.

## STEALING ONE'S THUNDER

Cherry, forty-two, is often preoccupied with her coworker's scheming. He frequently takes credit for her work and pushes her out of projects and accounts. She feels that he undermines her contributions to gain a better standing for himself. Each time something happens with him at work, she can't help but stay livid about it for days, so much so that her husband complains it's all she talks about at home.

Why is Cherry so preoccupied with work, even to the point where it spills over into her life at home, affecting her relationship with her husband? Circle the most correct answer.

1. Cherry has problems with affect regulation and can't self-soothe. She needs to go to therapy.
2. Cherry's husband is at fault—he can't find ways soothe her, and instead he makes her feel bad for being upset.
3. Cherry is too sensitive; she has an anxious attachment style, which makes her less of a team player. Instead of complaining to her husband, she should just find a solution.
4. Cherry feels that the workplace environment is unsafe, and hence, understandably, she can't leave it alone.

Cherry may have an anxious attachment style, but if she's right and her coworker is scheming against her, then she's picking up on something truly harmful to her career that needs to be addressed. Taking credit for other people's work and undermining them creates an unsafe, insecure environment that isn't good for anyone but is truly the worst possible scenario for someone with an anxious attachment style. Anxious people often have a sixth sense for detecting unsafe environments. The problem is, once their brain's threat system gets activated, it's very hard for them to turn it off. This can lead to obsessive focus on the problem, which in turn drains their productivity and creativity.

Cherry needs to either find a way to eliminate this threat at work, making sure this behavior stops, or leave and find another job. Her husband, though clearly not at fault, would be wise to try to support her and validate her feelings instead of making her feel even worse about the stressful work environment. Frankly, he can't completely soothe her in the face of her insecure situation, but he can certainly help mitigate it by acknowledging how difficult it is and having ample patience, understanding that someone with an anxious attachment style has no easy off switch. The correct answer is 4.

## GOING IT ALONE

Luke, thirty-two, recently started a new position where he oversees a few employees. Whereas before he worked mostly on his own and did quite well, in his current role his team struggles to submit deliverables on time because he insists on doing the more complicated tasks himself. He doesn't trust others to handle them. He feels the work never comes out as well as when he does it himself—and besides, he's always relied on his own wits. As a result, he ends up doing most of the heavy lifting, but the team still misses deadlines, despite his putting in hours upon hours at work. They often receive mixed performance reviews, and Luke worries he may not be promoted—or might even get laid off.

Why is Luke finding it so hard to delegate responsibility at work? Circle the most correct answer.

1. Luke should indeed be let go; he's an incompetent boss.
2. Luke has an avoidant attachment style, which emphasizes self-reliance. This stems from being neglected by his parents growing up. He can't help but fail at such a position.

3. Luke has an avoidant attachment style, and delegating work responsibilities as well as working in a collaborative team can be challenging, especially at first.

4. Luke's mixed performance reviews have nothing to do with his attachment style—he's simply not a team player.

This is a common struggle for people with avoidant attachment style. They prefer to rely on themselves. This can be great if the work you do is more solitary and requires the concerted effort of only one person—like Luke's former position—but it can be counterproductive if you're working with a team and need to delegate work. The problem can be mitigated by understanding your attachment style and training yourself to be aware of your tendency to go it alone. This will help you get out of your comfort zone and learn to share the workload with others. Research shows that just knowing about your avoidant or anxious tendencies will help you take small steps toward greater security, but the first step is to be aware of these tendencies. The correct answer, therefore, is 3. Answer 2 is incorrect because attachment styles are malleable and there's no proof that avoidant attachment stems from neglectful parenting.

## NOT FORGETTING, NOT FORGIVING

Mercedes, seventy-two, was upset that her close friend Minny didn't invite her to join a group of friends at lunch one day. It's been months now, and despite Minny's repeated apologies, Mercedes has continued giving her the cold shoulder. How does Mercedes's attachment style show up as she deals with the insult, even in the face of repeated apologies? Circle the most correct answer.

1. This has nothing to do with attachment styles. Mercedes suffered from the Cyberball effect and is right not to trust Minny anymore.

2. Mercedes is petty and holds a grudge. Why is she making a mountain out of a molehill?
3. Mercedes should give Minny another chance—especially in the face of what seems like a sincere apology for an accidental oversight.
4. Mercedes can't fully control her feelings about this upset, but with some awareness of her attachment style, and the use of a CARRP intervention, she might be able to preserve the friendship with Minny and make it more secure.

The correct answer is 4. What Mercedes experienced was the Cyberball effect in action. When we are excluded from a social event, it is simply painful. However, Mercedes's difficulty forgiving *does* relate to her attachment style. Research shows that people who score high in anxious attachment have a harder time letting go of a hurt such as the Cyberball effect. But the fact that Mercedes withdrew from the friendship and found herself unable to forgive Minny's Cyberball misstep despite repeated apologies suggests that Mercedes is fearful avoidant. She simply feels that she can't trust Minny anymore. How can she rebuild that trust?

A CARRP intervention may help Mercedes do just that. Minny may have apologized, but Mercedes—being a fearful avoidant—hesitates to forgive, fearing she may find herself Cyberballed by Minny again in some way. If Mercedes uses a CARRP intervention to educate Minny about the Cyberball effect (after all, many people aren't aware of the social pain it creates), and Minny conveys a genuine commitment to be hyperinclusive, the intervention could restore the trust in the friendship—and even deepen it.

## MICAH'S SECURE FASHION MAKEOVER

Micah was always anxious about how he looked. Before any event—whether it was work, a date, or just drinks with friends—he would agonize over his outfit. Was it too much? Did it hit the right balance between stylish and effortless? He loved fashion and had a great eye, but it became an obsession. He couldn't stop second-guessing himself.

He trawled online shops late at night, hunted down sample sales, and followed dozens of influencers whose curated feeds left him feeling both inspired and inadequate. God forbid someone saw him in the same outfit twice. His social media was filled with style posts, mirror selfies, and "what I wore" videos. He spent hours a day on these things.

Micah worked part time at a youth arts program in the city, teaching improv to LGBTQ+ teens and taking them to see performances. He'd sometimes share photos or short clips from their shows on his social media—always with the organization's permission and signed releases. His boyfriend at the time—a real jerk—accused Micah of using the students as a backdrop for his feed, suggesting that Micah didn't really care about the kids and that his posts were all for show. That comment really hurt Micah. And because, at the time, his anxious attachment made it hard to let go of the guy—or his snide comments—he set out to prove him wrong.

Micah took a full-time role at the program, built out a full curriculum, and poured hours upon hours into the work. He always felt he was doing it for the kids anyway—he never agreed with his boyfriend's take—but the criticism made him double down. At first, it was tough. Some of the teens pushed all of his buttons. One boy kept falling asleep in class, and it really upset him; he thought it was so disrespectful. Another girl constantly made snooty remarks.

In our work together, we talked about a secure pedagogic approach to education—meeting people where they are and finding ways to win them over. Micah discovered the boy was falling asleep a lot because of a medical issue he was struggling with. The remarks from the girl turned out to be a cry for help. With some one-on-one guidance, she began to thrive.

Over time, Micah's work with the kids—and finding his secure stance with them—transformed him. Gone was the preoccupation with the perfect outfit. He still liked to dress well, but it no longer felt urgent or all-consuming. His shopping habits dwindled to something much more manageable—he was too busy with his students and the work he cared about. His entire perspective on buying and consuming changed. He was also able to let go of his toxic relationship with relative ease.

"I'm so connected to these kids—I feel like my world is full," he said. "It made all that other stuff fade into the background. It just doesn't interest me the same way it used to."

Circle all the correct statements.

1. As Micah became more secure, his fashion sense changed.
2. Micah became more secure in part because he was able to leave a toxic relationship.
3. Being insecurely attached had nothing do to with Micah's obsession with fashion.
4. Micah's initial shopping habits were in line with his anxious attachment style.
5. Because Micah stopped shopping obsessively, he was able to become more secure.
6. Micah's relationship with the kids created an enriched environment that helped him become more secure.

The correct statements are 1, 2, 4, and 6.

Micah's transformation reflected a shift toward greater security, and it showed in his relationship to fashion—while he still appreciated designer brands and enjoyed dressing well, it no longer felt urgent or tied to his self-worth. Research shows that individuals with an anxious attachment style report significantly higher levels of materialism and are more likely to purchase status-signaling goods than those with a secure style. Anxious attachers may turn to clothing, social media, and consumerism to seek reassurance about their social standing. What ultimately helped Micah shift wasn't just leaving a toxic relationship (though that was a helpful step) but the meaningful connection he formed with his students. By showing up for them and finding his secure stance in the classroom, he created an enriched social environment that left him feeling grounded and fulfilled, making those old habits naturally lose their appeal and fade into the background.

## MIRABEL'S MULTIPLE "PERSONALITY DISORDERS"

Mirabel, forty-seven, struggles a lot with her seventeen-year-old son, Max. Max often lashes out at her and, after taking AP Psychology, has started diagnosing her with every condition he comes across. According to him, she's a rare blend of narcissistic, borderline, sociopathic, and histrionic personality disorders. He regularly tells her that she traumatized him, which hits her hard—especially since Mirabel feels she sacrificed so much for his sake, including staying in an unhappy marriage for fifteen years to keep the family together.

Mirabel has always had a short fuse. When she gets overwhelmed, she yells, telling Max he's ungrateful and screaming that if she's so awful, he should just go live with his father. "Just get out!" she yells again and again. Max usually storms off after these exchanges. Things have been even harder lately: Max has been having trouble falling asleep and has been refusing to get out of bed in the morning and go to school, which really pushes Mirabel's buttons.

Circle the most correct statement about Mirabel's interactions with Max.

1. Mirabel has a fearful avoidant attachment style, which makes her more likely to get swept up in difficult emotions and prone to outbursts. She just can't help it.

## TEST-DRIVE YOUR ATTACHMENT KNOWLEDGE

2. Mirabel may have a fearful avoidant attachment style—and perhaps other challenges as well—but that doesn't excuse her behavior. She needs to make sure she never blows up like that. It's unacceptable.

3. Mirabel should use the Stopping Yourself in Your Tracks and Apologizing method when she feels her temper starting to take over.

4. It's unacceptable for a son to speak to his mother like that. He should be called out for his rudeness.

While we don't know exactly which insecure attachment style Mirabel has—she may be anxious or fearful avoidant—it's clear that her relationship with her son reflects an insecure attachment pattern, which can stir up intense and difficult emotions. It's also true that she doesn't fully have control over her outbursts. With an insecure attachment style, it's genuinely hard to stay regulated when being challenged over and over again by your child.

However, the most correct statement is 3—Mirabel should use the Stopping Yourself in Your Tracks and Apologizing method when she feels her temper starting to take over. Option 3 offers a concrete solution. It gives Mirabel a tool she can use in the moment—even after an outburst has begun. She can still stop herself in her tracks, ask for help, and apologize to her son.

And while what her son says can be hurtful, and he should be told that, a secure person might find it amusing. He's diagnosed her with almost every possible disorder under the sun—a classic, ridiculous move for a psychology student. It's very common for teenagers to find fault with their parents. It's part of how they separate from them—a deactivating strategy, yes, but one that's completely developmentally normal. Still, it may be especially hard to bear for someone with insecure attachment.

What will help Mirabel is gaining a secure perspective on the situation on a regular basis—potentially through Secure Therapy. In the long run, this kind of treatment can help prevent those outbursts from happening in the first place.

---

As these scenarios show, attachment theory isn't just abstract—it's a practical lens for making sense of everyday relationships in all walks of life. Recognizing attachment patterns helps explain behaviors that might otherwise seem confusing or irrational. This awareness is the first step toward change. Attachment styles aren't fixed—with insight and practice, you can move toward greater security. Keep using the tools from this book, and you'll see a real shift in how you relate, connect, and thrive.

PART III

# The Secure Mind

Throughout this book you've been invited to look at your life through a scientific lens. In part 1, you learned what your brain needs to feel secure and were introduced to a set of tools to help get you there. In part 2, we looked at how each insecure attachment style can use this set of tools to move toward security. Now we'll explore ideas that can help you achieve a more secure mindset.

We're a meaning-based species. We thrive on exploring concepts and forming ideas, and whether we're aware of it or not, our well-being is often governed by certain assumptions we make about ourselves: where we come from, how we grew up, and our place in the world. This is, in fact, part of what attachment styles are about: They comprise a set of beliefs we have about ourselves and others. "I should only count on myself," "Others will not love me as much as I love them," "People are well meaning"—these are the basic assumptions people with different attachment styles make, which then affect how they experience the world.

In this final part of the book, we'll take a close look at some of these beliefs and assumptions, with the goal of reexamining them from a secure perspective. You'll be asked to reevaluate certain concepts and ideas that are ever present in the background of your life and decide if these ideas are helpful to you or if they get in the way of your security and happiness.

Here the focus will be on using specific scientific ideas as tools to help further fortify your secure mindset. I believe that certain scientific concepts are themselves powerful secure tools, and they form an integral part of Secure Therapy. As physicians, we're often taught how to help people heal through medications, but as a therapist I've discovered that adopting a secure worldview can influence our brains in ways no less powerful than taking a pill.

We'll start by discussing the concept of causality. We often think about things that happened to us in early childhood as decisive factors in shaping who we are and how our lives play out. But is this really the case? And can we ever know for sure?

# 10

# Causality: Recasting Your Past from a Secure Stance

"I think the root cause of all my problems today is the way my father treated me when I was a child."

"I'm always afraid that if I lose my temper with my boys, get upset, and yell or cry, it will scar them for life."

"I've had two terrible relationships, each lasting the better part of a decade. I now think something inside me is broken because I lived through my parents' bitter divorce when I was young. I feel like damaged goods."

We hear these assertions everywhere we turn. Statements of implied causality. Something that occurred to me in childhood is causing what is happening to me now. Or losing it with my kids will cause them to grow up damaged. Or because certain things have repeated in my life—two unfortunate relationships or a few jobs that weren't a good fit—it means there's a pattern, and these things are bound to happen again and again. But we scientists view causality differently, and I find that it can be quite beneficial, even freeing, to consider a scientific approach to causality both in therapy and in day-to-day life. I believe that viewing causality from this standpoint can be a powerful therapeutic vehicle that can lead to greater security.

I'll start by telling you the story of one of my patients, Anne.

## ANNE'S PREDICAMENT

Anne had always been afraid her father would die in a plane crash when he went away on business trips. Unfortunately, as a tech consultant, he had to travel almost weekly for his job. At times, Anne would clutch his leg as he was getting ready to leave, crying for him not to go. Her parents would hug her and gently reassure her that she had nothing to worry about, that he'd be back in no time, and that he'd call her every night from the road.

Anne's parents didn't fully take in the fact that she was suffering from debilitating separation anxiety, which is quite common in youth (about 4.5 percent of children aged five to thirteen are afflicted by separation anxiety disorder, and this prevalence increases to as much as 7.6 percent during the later adolescent years). They also didn't know that there are very effective treatments for separation anxiety, including cognitive behavioral therapy and medication or a combination of the two, that could have helped her immensely if only they had sought them out. To be fair, they are not alone in this lack of knowledge—studies show that as many as 80 percent of children with anxiety go undiagnosed and untreated.

After Anne's bouts of crying and protesting each time her father went away showed no effect, sensing her parents' exasperation, she gradually learned to keep most of her fears to herself. Despite spending many sleepless nights worried and scared when her father was away, she put on a brave face and behaved as if she weren't bothered by it anymore. Her parents didn't have a clue that underneath her calm facade she was still suffering inside.

## CAUSALITY: RECASTING YOUR PAST FROM A SECURE STANCE

As a grown-up, Anne questioned each of her romantic relationships. Years into living with someone, she would keep some of her personal items packed in boxes as though she might leave at any moment. For Anne, the decision to stay or go was almost a daily one.

In treatment we explored how, despite having loving parents, growing up with untreated separation anxiety led her to perceive even loving and kind relationships as a potential source of danger, pain, and unease. The terror she experienced as a child left an emotional equation in her mind: Closeness equals danger, and she should not let anyone in. Just as she once hid her struggles from her parents, Anne felt compelled to conceal her doubts and fears from her partners. In her adult relationships she replayed the same isolation she had known as a child, when she bottled up her dread each time her father left.

Over time in our sessions, Anne gradually became more comfortable with emotional closeness within the therapeutic relationship. She grew more open and less guarded, which, in turn, helped her feel safer being vulnerable with her partner and sharing her fears, worries, and uncertainty. Her partner was patient and supportive; he could see that this repetitive pattern had nothing to do with him, and he wanted to help her. We worked on her unpacking her boxes and taking other small actions to make their place her home. All these interventions led to her feeling more at ease in her relationship, and she was able to let down her defenses and accept the support of a loving partner. It took some time, but eventually Anne found an emotional place where she felt safe and heard, and with that, her doubts about staying in the relationship subsided.

My view of Anne's circumstances, drawing a connection between her childhood symptoms and her adult predicament, is commonplace in psychological treatment. When I first learned to conduct psychodynamic psychotherapy, we were taught to recognize causal inferences from childhood to adulthood, as I did with Anne. Establishing this link was also emphasized in my training with my own analyst, who showed me how some of my early experiences helped shape my adult view of the world.

However, it was only once I became a full-fledged scientist—in addition to being a clinician and a therapist—that I came to appreciate how difficult it is to establish true causality, and this has had a profound impact on my work with patients. Let me explain.

## SETTING UP YOUR OWN EXPERIMENT

Say you conduct an experiment on laboratory mice. You make a hypothesis: Giving omega-3 fatty acid to young mice will improve their memory as adults. You then give a group of young mice a diet enriched with omega-3 and have a control group that receives regular chow. You wait until they reach adulthood (in mice, two to three months), and then you test their memory and cognition. You let them run in a maze shaped like the letter *T* with the food located on the right end of the *T* arm and examine how quickly they learn to make the correct turn to get the food. You have them swim in a large tub of water that has a secret sunken island they can stand on and measure the amount of time and number of trials it takes for them to consistently remember where the island is. (Mice don't particularly like swimming, so as soon as they know the location of the sunken island, the next time you put them in the tub they will go directly there.) You discover that mice that were given the diet enriched in omega-3 fatty acid learn to locate food in a maze and memorize the whereabouts of the sunken island in the water tub much faster than the regular-chow mice. Did you prove that more omega-3 in the mice's diet causes better memory? Not entirely. You showed an interesting correlation, but nothing more. For instance, maybe better food leads to less infighting and competition among the mice, which in turn leads to a better learning environment. Or maybe omega-3 lowered the mice's anxiety, and that—not improved memory—is what led to better test performance. There are so many variables to consider that it is difficult to prove causality in such a way.

When you conduct experiments in lab mice, you become even more

## CAUSALITY: RECASTING YOUR PAST FROM A SECURE STANCE

humble in making causal inferences when you work with humans. You see, lab mice are nearly identical genetically. Through generations of inbreeding, scientists have created essentially the closest thing to a colony of mouse clones. The surprising thing is that when you work with these almost-identical mice, you discover how differently they behave despite their genetic similarities. For example, if you introduce a bully into the cage of young lab mice, in a test called the social defeat paradigm, some will grow up to be fearful and depressed, while others will show remarkable resilience and behave like mice that grew up without the adverse early life experience. It's remarkable to see that even animals that are nearly genetically identical respond very differently to early adversity. There could be many reasons why some mice are more resilient than others; it could stem from variations in the womb environment, maternal behavior, interactions with cage mates, or simply chance, such as whom the bully targets more. But it's very hard—in fact, it is almost impossible—to pinpoint the causes in these mice, let alone in humans.

So if mice can show remarkably different responses to early life experiences, it's reasonable to say that drawing precise causal inferences from childhood to adulthood in humans—who vary genetically a great deal and have far more sophisticated brains—is quite impossible.

## CAUTIOUSLY CAUSAL

Since I became a scientist, I have adopted a more careful approach to the use of causality in my practice. I continue to use causal inferences with my patients, but I use language that is more suggestive than certain. I might say that there are potential echoes from the past in their current experience, while cautioning my patients to treat these connections with a grain of salt. I urge them to view these echoes as a narrative to adopt if it helps them but to abandon that narrative if they find that it does not. Some find it comforting to think that because something happened to them in childhood, they have a tendency to respond in a certain way in the here and now. They feel they can work through it and get better. Others experience it more as an impediment. They think, "If I'm like this now because this happened to me in childhood, I'm broken or at least defective. I was wronged, and now I'm doomed."

In Anne's case, we can't prove that it was her separation anxiety in childhood that prevented her from settling down with someone. I've had other patients who suffered from terrible separation anxiety as children but went on to form exceptionally close bonds with their significant others. Also, Anne had relatives who exhibited fearful avoidant tendencies like her own but didn't have separation anxiety, so perhaps there's a genetic component. We would never know for sure. And, truth be told, this causal explanation would not have changed her treatment. The behavioral aspects of the therapy, including the unpacking of boxes, for example, and the cognitive and emotional components that led Anne to feel more comfortable expressing her thoughts and feelings were not related to the causal inference of her early experience with her father.

The fact is, many of the proven-to-work, evidence-based psychotherapies don't rely on examining childhood events as part of the treatment. For example, cognitive behavioral therapy (CBT) for depression focuses on dissecting the relationship between mood, thoughts, and behaviors. Interpersonal therapy, another evidence-based treatment for depression, targets specific recent events that may have triggered your symptoms and works on improving your close relationships to boost your mood. Behavioral activation, another treatment for depression, successfully helps patients improve by encouraging them to engage in meaningful and rewarding activities. Exposure treatments focus on the thing or things that make you nervous and uncomfortable regardless of any diagnosis you may have received—whether obsessive-compulsive disorder, post-traumatic stress disorder, or an anxiety disorder. These treatments gradually expose you to the source of your fears to help you conquer them, thereby alleviating your symptoms. Notably, none of these evidence-based treatments

## CAUSALITY: RECASTING YOUR PAST FROM A SECURE STANCE

emphasize dissecting early childhood experiences as a core part of getting better.

This is not to say that there's no place for recounting childhood experiences in therapy. Even though we cannot accurately draw causal explanations from childhood to adulthood, the simple act of recounting childhood memories can have a powerful effect. From a neuroscience perspective, recounting childhood memories in a safe environment leads to a phenomenon called memory reconsolidation, which in turn may afford you the opportunity to review and edit key memories, even those from your distant past—in effect changing them forever.

Think about a time you revisited a place you remembered from childhood—a huge lobby of a building or a large town square. As an adult, you suddenly see it as right-sized—it is not so enormous anymore; your memory of the place is edited. Whenever you think of it again, you now see it from this new perspective rather than from the original larger-than-life point of view you had as a child. You still remember that it used to look bigger to you, but now the memory itself has been edited, forever altering the image in your mind.

In the presence of secure relationships—and not just in therapy—your brain reshapes your memory and perception of past events. Just as your memory of the lobby changes once you've seen it again as an adult, memories of painful events—like a time your father treated you terribly—can also shift when recalled in the presence of someone secure. Recalling the events while feeling safe in the here and now can take some of the sting out of it and start to reshape how you see it. Given the right secure environment, you may begin to shift your view. You might see your father as a victim of his own difficult circumstances and highlight in your mind things he did that may have helped you. This can interrupt the memories of the difficult experiences, recasting them in a new light and, in essence, lessening their hold on you.

There's another important aspect of recalling childhood memories in treatment that is worth considering. In psychotherapy, one of the most important factors for treatment success is the quality of the relationship between the therapist and the patient. If a patient feels that they can trust their therapist, they can make great strides regardless of which particular treatment modality their therapist is using. I find that listening to and recounting childhood memories, both happy and sad, helps patient and therapist connect on a deeper level in therapy. How often do you get to think about your childhood, let alone recount it, with someone who cares and wants to help? Retelling these experiences can provide an important vehicle for forming a strong therapeutic bond, which is crucial for treatment success.

## CAUSALITY, ATTACHMENT STYLES, AND BECOMING SECURE

Many people draw a causal link between the attachment style they had as a child and the one they have as an adult. But here again, the story is more complicated. Studies show only a weak correlation between childhood and adult attachment styles. Many children who are anxious and avoidant grow up to be secure, and many secure kids will grow up to develop insecure attachment styles.

Furthermore, attachment research views the teenage years as a critical period in which attachment styles can morph and change to the point that our adult attachment style might have little resemblance to the style we had as a child. This makes sense, because it's a period when social allegiance changes dramatically.

In our teenage years we begin to place a lot more emphasis on our peers, and these new relationships can change our attachment style, making us more or less secure. At the same time, the adolescent brain undergoes dramatic changes involving the pruning and reconfiguring of neural pathways. Essentially, the brain is demolishing many little roads in the service of constructing massive communication megahighways. These extensive changes

# CAUSALITY: RECASTING YOUR PAST FROM A SECURE STANCE

in the brain allow for the adoption of new ideas and new belief systems that can be quite different from those of the household we grew up in—another reason why attachment styles might change during that time.

Adolescence can be seen as a period when a complete remapping and repointing of relationships occurs. If you recall, this is what happened to Eric, whose story I shared in chapter 3. In his late teens he underwent a major shift in worldview and attachment style as a result of his treatment with his therapist, Deborah, who helped him learn new ways of thinking and relating.

Adolescence isn't the only time in our lives when attachment styles have the potential to change; in fact, they change throughout our lives. This makes sense from an evolutionary standpoint: We need to remain adaptive to our social circumstances. *Homo sapiens* is an übersocial species, and its social adaptiveness is one of its greatest strengths. You're much more malleable than you probably give yourself credit for—you are the product of a mosaic of influences and have a repertoire of ways to respond to a world that continually evolves. This social neuroplasticity, the very fact that even your memories of past events are malleable, is great news. It gives you the opportunity to change and heal and find a better outcome for yourself, given the right environment.

## A FEW FINAL WORDS

I wrote this chapter for those of you who are holding on to a particular causal explanation that may not be serving you. Maybe you feel bad about events in your childhood that you have come to believe are stopping you from making progress in your life, and you resent your parents for it. Or perhaps you are a parent, and you blame yourself for things that transpired with your children as they grew up that you believe have led to difficulties later in their lives. I want to tell you, as someone who's seen much simpler hypotheses about and explanations of mouse behavior fly out the window, that there are too many variables to consider when it comes to finding causality in the behaviors, thoughts, and feelings of a single human being. If any particular explanation is helpful for you, keep it. But if it brings you unhappiness or pain or is holding you back from healing, think about reexamining it with this information in mind.

There are many paths for positive change, and a good number of them lie in the here and now.

## CAUSALITY WORKSHOP: THINK LIKE A SCIENTIST

### Jeremy's Alcohol Problem

Jeremy always believed he became an alcoholic because his father had been harsh and authoritarian during his childhood. His father never drank while Jeremy was growing up—he had given up alcohol after a series of troubling incidents before Jeremy was born and stayed sober until his last breath.

What's the most likely reason Jeremy had alcohol problems?

1. His father's stern behavior.//
2. His father's genes.
3. Random chance.
4. He was self-medicating.

The most likely reason is number 2, his father's genes. His father swore off drinking because it got him into trouble, which is a red flag for having alcoholism. Though his father was able to quit drinking, a family history of alcoholism has been shown to significantly increase one's likelihood of becoming an alcoholic. However, a history of trauma and comorbid mental disorders, potentially leading to self-medicating, are also factors that may contribute to alcoholism. In this case, the most glaring reason appears to be the family history.

## Identifying Presumed Causality in Your Life

List causal inferences you use in your life:

I think that I am _____

because of _____.

Is there an alternative explanation? If so, list it here:

_____

In what ways is this causal inference helping me?

_____

In what way is it hindering me?

_____

Is this inference necessary for my understanding of myself and how I interact with the people around me?

_____

Does using the alternative explanation help me?

_____

## SECURE

Are there solutions in the here and now that can help me regardless of the causal explanation?

---

# 11

# The Comparing and Collaborative Brain: Finding the Right People to Count On

You're probably doing it right now—comparing yourself to someone else without even realizing it. At work, you know what your own workload looks like, but you're also keenly aware of whether you're working more or less than your coworkers. You hope you're being compensated fairly and that others at your level aren't getting more. In your personal life, you're likely aware of how you measure up to your friends and family across a wide range of factors—money, education, connections, number of children, and so on.

As social mammals, our brains are wired to compare. We're programmed to check: Where do I stand in relation to others? Am I getting my fair share? Am I missing out on something? So much of our internal experience is influenced by what others are doing. What's more, it turns out that this comparison shapes how our brain perceives the world.

This was vividly demonstrated in an impressive study by Klaus Fliessbach and colleagues from the Life & Brain center in Bonn. Two participants were scanned in functional MRI machines side by side while playing a video game. In the game, they stood to win either thirty euros or sixty euros. The machine measured activity in the ventral striatum—the area of the brain that is activated when one receives a reward, whether money, a drug, an exercise high, or even candy. The participants were able to see their own score and winnings as well as their mate's.

Remarkably, the brain's reward area was activated only when participants won more money than their counterparts. Winning money alone—normally enough to trigger that area—didn't do it if you were aware that someone nearby won more! Similar results have been found in other studies in both men and women. Together these findings show that even though we are often told that we should not compare ourselves to others—that we should be content with what we've got—our brains don't work that way. In fact, our whole experience is relational; it doesn't exist in a vacuum. *We can't help but compare.*

Adam experienced this firsthand. He was renting an apartment in a luxury high-rise overlooking an even more extravagant building. He loved his apartment—it was spacious, with high-end finishes, and even had a personal sauna. Yet through his window, Adam could see that the apartments across from him were much grander, and he often found himself daydreaming about winning the lottery and moving into one of them.

When Adam's lease ran out, he moved to another building a few blocks away with condos that were less upscale—gone was the sauna, and in general, his space was less grand. Instead of overlooking the luxury condos, the new apartment faced the street and a well-kept city-sponsored retirement housing complex. To his surprise, once he acclimated to his new place, Adam discovered that he felt happier and more content in his new home than he had in his old apartment. He also stopped getting lottery tickets and fantasizing about buying a fancy condo. It barely crossed his mind.

It's important to consider that your sense of reward is not determined by your brain in isolation; rather, it is dependent on the information your neurocircuitry is comparing it to. One can't help but wonder: What is the logic behind such a system? Wouldn't it be better to be satisfied with your own winnings from the video game, regardless of what your partner won?

At first glance, this comparing neurocircuitry seems petty and unhelpful. To understand how it can be beneficial—and, more important, how you can harness it to become more secure—let's look at comparison through an evolutionary lens.

## THE EVOLUTIONARY WISDOM BEHIND PICKING ON SOMEONE YOUR OWN SIZE

You're at a Yankees game, rallying for your team and hurling derisive, obnoxious comments at the opposing side. You're not exactly the biggest or strongest person in the crowd, but your passion for your team is undeniable. Eventually, you get on the nerves of someone sitting nearby, and he asks you to stop heckling his team. You ignore him and keep going, not wanting to back down. At some point he gets up and says, "That's it. Let's take it outside, buddy. I'll teach you a thing or two about my team."

You know you're in over your head, but you're not too worried. Your best friend, who's sitting next to you, stands up. At six foot four and built like a mountain, he towers over the other guy. "If you want to get to him, you'll have to go through me first," he says. The other guy glances at your friend and sits down without a word.

The guy rooting for the other team was wise to back off. His comparing neurocircuitry saved him from a potentially dangerous run-in with someone much bigger and stronger than he was. His quick assessment and retreat aren't unlike responses we see in other competitive species.

Indeed, many animals have evolved a neurocircuitry designed to compare themselves with others of their own species in terms of size and strength. For example, red deer compare their roars to those of others of their kind to determine whether it's wise to fight. The bigger the deer, the deeper the roar; if you're a tenor, and therefore smaller, challenging a baritone will probably lead to getting your antlers kicked, so why even go there? The same is true for other competitive species, too, such as baboons, and even for nonmammalian species—some lizards apparently have push-up contests to help determine who's a worthy opponent, rendering many potentially harmful physical altercations moot.

In humans and many other social animals, an important neuronal upgrade is the ability to assess not just strength, worth, or merit but also how well others will collaborate with you. This is particularly true in species that collaborate widely, even outside their immediate kinship—wolves, rats, some birds, and humans. This more advanced, sophisticated form of comparison allows us to gauge how well someone will work with us to get a job done—just as having a big and brawny friend at your side can make you behave more boldly.

Having good collaborative relationships helps you in all areas of life—from parenting to friendships to work and creative endeavors in general. In addition, if you have an insecure attachment style, engaging in these collaborations can lead to another outcome—it can help you and your brain take the necessary leap of faith to become more secure.

This was certainly true for Nina, who went through several doctors until she found one who could truly partner with her—a search that turned out to be lifesaving.

Nina had a chronic medical condition that started in her late teens. When she moved to New York, she looked for a doctor who could help her manage her illness. In the period prior to her move, she was in and out of the hospital every few weeks with frequent life-threatening flare-ups. Once in New York, Nina was determined to get her symptoms under control. In her first appointment with the new physician, she presented him with material she had found online, but he dismissed it as unhelpful, giving the impression that he knew what he was doing and she shouldn't question him. When she shared additional information that he was unaware of, she could tell it annoyed him and that he felt threatened by her inquisitiveness. Nina decided to try someone else, but that doctor was even worse. She had to wait as long as an hour to see her, and she felt the doctor was not knowledgeable enough.

# THE COMPARING AND COLLABORATIVE BRAIN

Then Nina met Dr. Lee and that changed everything. Dr. Lee had a vast breadth of knowledge; you could tell just by talking to him that he was a walking medical encyclopedia. But he was also easygoing and open, eager to learn from her whenever she shared something new. In fact, he would routinely thank her for bringing valuable information to his attention. Nina stuck with Dr. Lee for years to come, and it paid off. She had far fewer flare-ups than she'd had in the past, and when she did get sick, Dr. Lee helped manage her symptoms early and at home, sparing her the need for inpatient hospitalization. She was so happy that she hadn't given up on trying to find the right doctor and was grateful for their teamwork, which not only kept her out of the hospital but also gave her her life back.

Nina's story shows how the right partnership can be lifesaving. Not all collaborations are made the same. Some are exceptionally good, and others falter. It's crucial to determine who's worthy of your attention and efforts. A lot is at stake. When you invest your time, energy, and resources in someone, does it drain you with little return or do they give back in kind so that, together, you can grow? Surrounding yourself with the right people can make or break the course of your life.

## OUR BRAINS ARE WIRED TO RESIST UNCOLLABORATIVE COLLABORATIONS

You're playing a game with a partner. All the winnings go to your mate, and they get to decide how much they will share with you. However, you're not entirely helpless in this situation. If you disagree with their allocation of the prize, you have veto power. If you refuse the funds they send your way, the whole prize is eliminated and no one gets a cent. Say you play together, and you win ten dollars. The other person gives you one dollar and keeps the rest. What would you do?

It turns out that most people will refuse the one dollar and prefer that everyone loses rather than accept what they deem an unfair situation—

even though on the surface it seems illogical. After all, one dollar is better than nothing.

The reason we react in ways that seem irrational is because these collaborative assessments don't only happen in the analytical part of the brain. They also take place in the limbic system—the part responsible for our emotions and basic drives. Before we even have a chance to think things through, a surge of emotion takes over and leads us to reject the unfair proposal. It happens almost instinctively.

As a creature equipped with this neural wiring, you tend to cooperate until you perceive an imbalance in rewards, which might lead to a form of revolt. This behavior is not unique to humans; it has been observed in primates, dogs, birds, and rats. For instance, two capuchin monkeys will each happily collaborate with an experimenter, trading a pebble for a slice of cucumber, until one observes the other receiving a grape instead—a more coveted treat. At that point, the slighted monkey will stop collaborating and angrily shake the enclosure, demanding their fair share.

You perform cooperative assessments all the time, and they affect your interactions with everyone around you. They also impact attraction. Research shows that life partners who feel supported find their partners more attractive and are drawn to them more.

Because this assessment happens instinctively, you may find yourself confused about why you are responding in a certain way, distancing yourself from friends or family or shutting down at work. But inside, sometimes unbeknownst to you, you intuit that continuing to cooperate with a given person or institution is not worth it. And if you try to ignore that feeling, it will add a level of stress to your life.

This is what happened to Shawn. Shawn's boss was notorious for his bullying tactics. He routinely took credit for other people's contributions, and Shawn never knew whether he'd be the target of a snide remark or unexpected praise. He also had to stay on guard to make sure his boss wasn't assigning parts of his project to others—a tactic he used to stoke competition within the team. Shawn felt trapped; he needed to complete the project to advance his career, so he couldn't walk away. Over time, the toxic environment wore him down. He became increasingly anxious and despondent. On weekends, he'd sit at home frozen, dreading Monday's return to the office. Eventually, it got so bad he had to start taking medication.

It's important to emphasize that we can tolerate situations that our collaborative neurocircuitry deems unfavorable, but it comes with a significant emotional toll. It's not just a cold calculation—it affects core areas of the brain that are related to our basic emotions and determine our overall sense of well-being and security.

## SECURE COLLABORATION VERSUS BOUNDARY SETTING

In my talks, to drive an important message home, I often say that as an attachment clinician, I don't believe in boundaries. But before you get all riled up about this admittedly provocative statement, let me explain the attachment rationale.

In secure relationships, setting boundaries is rarely necessary. When two people are attuned to each other and form a secure collaboration, the right give-and-take just happens organically, behind the scenes. Secures are skilled at employing theory of mind—the ability to put themselves in someone else's shoes and respond to their wants and needs—and importantly, it's a two-way street. Secure relationships are like a waltz: One person takes a step forward, the other takes a step back, and the duo dances in perfect unison.

As opposed to setting boundaries, where one person dictates their terms expecting others to fall in line, in a secure collaboration, whether with a partner, a friend, or a colleague, each person's needs are met almost seamlessly, and people quickly figure out how to work together. Even when they disagree, secures excel at accommodating each other. For secures, finding common ground often works better than drawing a line in the sand and telling others they can't cross it.

You may ask, isn't it necessary to set boundaries if people aren't secure, that is, they're not CARRP? If an organic CARRP collaboration isn't working, even after CARRP interventions, it's a sign that the collaboration isn't optimal. You may choose to give it less primacy in your life—lower the volume on it. Once you disengage like that, setting a boundary becomes less important, because you will have fewer interactions with this person and more with others who are secure. From an attachment perspective, a CARRP intervention is the closest alternative to boundary setting. But the goal is different: Rather than protecting yourself or drawing a line, you're inviting the other person to interact more securely. You're not shaping the relationship simply to suit your needs—you're modeling security and seeing if they can meet you there.

In fact, I find that the strongest kind of relationships are the ones where people try to outdo each other in being helpful and caring; that's when you know things are working well and the need for boundaries has become simply unnecessary. As we saw in chapter 4, the more connected you feel, the less energy your brain needs to complete tasks. Setting boundaries may interfere with that seamless relationship flow. From that perspective, setting boundaries can actually tax your brain.

One couple I know always tries to outshine each other in the best possible way. Any opportunity to help the other person or contribute to the household is seen as a chance to one-up their partner. There's never a question of who does what and for whom—things get done, because they try to do as much as possible for each other without expecting anything in return. And they frequently thank each other for doing simple chores around the house: "Thanks for doing the dishes," "Thank you for doing the laundry," "Thanks for taking the dog out," "Thanks for making breakfast."

## THE COMPARING AND COLLABORATIVE BRAIN

When both people are CARRP and give their best, a careful, secure balance is created, and the need for setting a boundary simply never arises.

### Why a Secure Collaboration Is Better Than Setting Boundaries

| SECURE INTERACTIONS VERSUS BOUNDARY SETTING | | BENEFIT |
|---|---|---|
| Secure interactions create a respectful dynamic that focuses on reciprocal care rather than the needs of just one person. | → | This leads to relationships thriving because the needs of both sides are considered and respected. |
| Secure interactions emphasize goodwill between people rather than putting up barriers to connection. | → | This leads to open communication, mutual understanding, and a feeling of closeness. |
| Secure interactions allow for flexibility and nuance in different contexts rather than blanket rules. | → | This often sparks more creative and expansive solutions, preventing relationship stagnation and allowing both people to grow in sync. |

## THE CHERRY ON TOP: WHEN COLLABORATIVE ASSESSMENTS WORK

Beyond the obvious benefits of a good collaboration, working well with others has a tremendously positive effect on the human brain. Several studies have shown that when we engage in effective collaboration, our brain harmonizes with the brains of our collaborators, creating a phenomenon called collective effervescence. With that comes a feeling of contentment and happiness as well as markedly improved performance and productivity.

One such famous collaboration happened between Daniel Kahneman and Amos Tversky, two social scientists whose groundbreaking partnership led to the birth of the field of behavioral economics and a Nobel Prize.

Danny and Amos were opposites: Danny was anxious and skeptical; Amos was confident and bold. Danny studied visual distortions; Amos studied decision-making. When they joined forces, their ideas fused into something entirely new. Through a decade of walking, talking, thinking, and writing together, they produced eight seminal papers that led to a complete paradigm shift in the understanding of how we assess information. They proved that our brains make systematic, predictable errors—not just in what we see (Danny's original expertise) but in how we think (Amos's area of research). Their ideas changed psychology and economics forever.

But even their extraordinary collaboration frayed. Amos received more accolades and moved to a top-tier institution, and their relationship soured. Eventually, they stopped speaking. Danny's collaborative circuitry struggled to accept the imbalance.

When Amos was dying, they reconnected. After his death, Danny won the Nobel Prize for their joint work. He later wrote the bestselling book *Thinking, Fast and Slow*, which popularized their ideas around the world.

Their story is a reminder: Our brains don't easily tolerate unequal recognition, even in the greatest of partnerships. Had Danny and Amos been more aware of the forces at play, they might have been more careful to protect their collaboration. Incredible partnerships are worth their weight in gold—and they're worth preserving.

When a collaboration ends, it can be painful. Our brain's attachment system is wired to hold on to close connections. But the ability to form social bonds never leaves us. Given the right circumstances, new, meaningful collaborations can take root. It's one of our greatest strengths as a species: finding the people who bring out the best in us—and doing the same in return.

In my own life, I've been fortunate to have had incredible collaborations that enabled me to evolve and grow. In the introduction to this book, I told you about Jimmy, my mentor who taught me how to become a neuroscientist. As I was writing these lines, I couldn't help but remember a time when I was falling behind on a grant proposal I was preparing to submit to the National Institutes of Health. It was Thursday, and the deadline, Monday, was right around the corner. Jimmy made a suggestion: "Pack a bag and come stay with us for the weekend. We'll work together and get it done." And so I did.

He lived on the Upper West Side, in an apartment overlooking Central Park and the Museum of Natural History. We sat there and worked on the proposal all weekend while I occasionally looked up to admire the view from the window. Come Monday, the application was ready to go.

By understanding and working with—rather than against—our comparing nature, we can build more satisfying relationships and create environments where our social brain can work to its fullest capacity. Remember the discussion in chapter 4 about energy and the brain, and how the solution for a more efficient brain lies outside us, with the people we interact with? Here this comes into full practice. The better the collaboration, the more efficient your brain's use of energy is and the more you can achieve.

In the following section is a questionnaire I devised, the Collaborative Assessment Scale, that will help you carefully assess the various collaborations in your life to ensure that you invest in ones that are more secure.

## COLLABORATIVE ASSESSMENT WORKSHOP

### How Secure Are Your Collaborations?
### The Collaborative Assessment Scale (CAS)

The collaborative assessment neurocircuitry can run rampant in your emotional world, making you unhappy and insecure. However, you can take the bull by the horns and harness it to help you become more secure.

First, assess your collaboration with the people in your life and assign a score to each relationship. Then examine how much time and effort you devote to these relationships. Wherever feasible, you can then set your relationship priorities, giving primacy to the people in your life who score the highest.

To put it into practice, use the Collaborative Assessment Scale (CAS) below. For each statement, circle your level of agreement from 1 (strongly disagree) to 5 (strongly agree) regarding a specific person in your life. To calculate the total score, add up the individual scores for each question. The total score indicates the overall quality of the collaboration in the relationship.

**Strongly Disagree    1   2   3   4   5    Strongly Agree**

| QUESTION | RESPONSE |
|---|---|
| This person has my well-being in mind. | 1 2 3 4 5 |
| This person shows willingness to both give and receive. | 1 2 3 4 5 |
| The effort I invest in this relationship is sustainable (not too draining). | 1 2 3 4 5 |
| The relationship feels fair and balanced. | 1 2 3 4 5 |
| I feel heard, seen, and valued in this relationship. | 1 2 3 4 5 |
| I am making the other person feel heard, seen, and valued. | 1 2 3 4 5 |
| This person refrains from Cyberballing or stillfacing behaviors in our interactions. | 1 2 3 4 5 |
| This person is open to other points of view and is willing to find common ground. | 1 2 3 4 5 |

**Strongly Disagree**     **1   2   3   4   5**     **Strongly Agree**

| QUESTION | RESPONSE |
|---|---|
| This person has my back. | 1 2 3 4 5 |
| The SIMIs with this person are mostly positive. | 1 2 3 4 5 |
| I feel emotionally stable in this relationship. | 1 2 3 4 5 |
| This person does not intentionally do things to punish me or "teach me a lesson." | 1 2 3 4 5 |
| This person is CARRP with me. | 1 2 3 4 5 |
| I am CARRP with this person. | 1 2 3 4 5 |
| Overall, this person is worth collaborating with. | 1 2 3 4 5 |
|  | Total Score: |

## Scoring

**0–25:** The relationship is fraught with problems. You don't feel safe, as there are frequently unpleasant surprises. There is a lack of effective give-and-take, which crushes the collaborative spirit. There certainly is no easy relationship flow. Instead, the relationship is hard work and requires a lot of energy. You may want to think about whether collaborating with this person is worth it for you, whether it can be improved, or if you need to deprioritize the relationship.

**26–50:** A score in this range suggests that the collaboration is not bad, but depending on what you expect from the relationship, there might be room for improvement. Some aspects of the collaboration may be working quite well, but others get in the way of a smoother exchange. At the end of the day, you will need to come to a decision: Can I improve on what's here? And if not, is the relationship working for me or is it taking up too much space in my life? Do I need to divert some of the energy and resources that I devote to this relationship toward a higher-scoring one? You will probably find that you have quite a few relationships that score in this range, and depending on the context, it may be fine. However, if the collaboration leaves you hurt and unhappy more often than not, you will want to reshuffle your relationship priorities.

**51–75:** The collaboration is working well to extremely well. No relationship is perfect, but it seems that you are for the most part helpful to each other. However, there may be some important elements lacking. For example, non-CARRP interactions are taxing on the brain, so even if there are other positive collaboration elements, you'll want to address a low CARRP score (please refer to the two items before the last one in the questionnaire, which measure CARRP).

In general, the higher the score, the better the collaboration. When you reach 60 and above, that usually means that you've hit the cream of the crop of an effective collaboration. You have great back-and-forth with this person. You're fortunate to have them in your life.

Now complete the questionnaire for some of your most important relationships, whether with family, colleagues, or friends. Then, using the scores, create a closeness hierarchy.

First, write down, in the left column under "Whom I Feel the Closest To," the people you feel the closest to, in descending order—the person you feel closest to in the first spot, the next closest in second place, and so on. Then, in the adjacent column under "CAS Score," fill in each person's score.

The higher the CAS score, the higher on the list the relationship should appear. If there's a discrepancy between your sense of closeness and the CAS score, you may want to reshuffle your relationship priorities.

This kind of social reorganization—emphasizing the bonds where the back-and-forth flows more easily—can help you achieve greater security.

|   | WHOM I FEEL THE CLOSEST TO | CAS SCORE |
|---|---|---|
| 1 | | |
| 2 | | |
| 3 | | |
| 4 | | |
| 5 | | |
| 6 | | |

## Quiz: Test Your Collaboration Assessment Knowledge

**Missy's Predicament**
Missy contracted mono and had to stay home from school for a few weeks. During that time, her friend Mallory completely dropped the ball on her. Mallory barely answered her texts and never came to visit. After Missy recovered, they resumed their usual friendship; Mallory even sort of apologized, explaining that while Missy was sick, she was really overwhelmed with things and just shut down. But Missy discovered that, despite the apology, and even though they did resume their friendship, something inside her had changed. She was surprised by how much the enthusiasm she'd had for their friendship had faded, and doing things together just seemed less fun. "Why am I making such a big deal out of this?" she kept asking her mother. "We were such good friends. We share a lot of

common interests, and she did kind of apologize. So why is part of me rejecting her now?"

What is your best assessment of the situation?

1. Missy's inability to forgive stems from early childhood trauma and is now displaced onto her relationship with Mallory.

2. Missy is a person who holds a grudge and struggles to forgive. She will have a hard time managing life as an adult.

3. Missy's brain received new information about Mallory when she was sick and now can't just ignore it and go back to the way things were.

4. Missy's mother should tell her daughter to snap out of it and double down on her friendship efforts with Mallory—do more things together until this feeling passes and they can be friends again.

The correct answer is 3.

It is often assumed that we can forgive and forget just because we want to. But our brains beg to differ. As you now know, the comparative assessment process often happens instinctively in our emotional brain; we don't have complete control over it. In Missy's case, her neurocircuitry implicitly encoded a lasting lesson—this person may not be there when I need them—and she couldn't easily disregard it. It's like learning to ride a bike and then trying to forget. The fact is that Missy received new information about her friend and, based on that information, decided she couldn't fully trust or count on Mallory.

### The Unfair Promotion

Cindy was working for a large consulting firm and was happy with her job. She was a hard worker and ambitious about advancing in the corporation. Then Stefan came into the picture. Stefan was a more recent hire, but to the amazement of everyone on the team, their boss fell in love with him. She spent a good half hour at his desk every day chatting him up, gave him the most interesting projects, and promoted him without merit. Cindy found herself losing interest in her projects and instead spending time online searching for other jobs. Without realizing it, she joined the ranks of the quiet quitters; even though she showed up at meetings and went through the motions, in spirit, she was no longer there.

How would you assess this situation?

1. Cindy should rise above it. Sometimes these injustices happen at work. It's not a reason to disengage. She will get her promotion in due time.

2. Cindy has an excessive need for reassurance and attention and that hurts her job performance.

3. Cindy's collaborative assessment neurocircuitry is engaging her emotional brain, making it harder for her to find the motivation to do her job.

4. Cindy is petty and competitive beyond reason. Sometimes bosses like certain employees and promote them. He may be a rising star, and she's just jealous.

The correct answer is 3. Cindy's perception of an unfair collaborative assessment triggers an emotional response, leading her to disengage from work. This is hard to overcome, as it is deeply rooted in our social wiring and is not entirely within our control. It is not a case of needing excessive reassurance; if indeed the promotion is without merit, it creates a strong feeling of injustice that's hard to shake off.

If you feel that you're being unfairly treated at work, you lose your zeal and drive to produce and succeed. But it can be remedied, as we will see from the case of Tamara.

### Start-Up Trouble

Tamara, the chief scientific officer at a promising biotech start-up, had been instrumental in developing the company's groundbreaking biological invention. As the company moved through multiple investment rounds, she realized that she'd been left behind—her equity stake had been diluted much more than those of the other executives, who were closer to the CEO.

During a meeting with the CEO, Tamara raised the issue, pointing out that while other executives had received additional equity grants during recent funding rounds, she hadn't been offered the same opportunity. She emphasized her critical role in the company's success and the potential impact on her long-term commitment.

The CEO acknowledged her concerns but explained that the decision was based on investor demands and market standards for similar roles. He promised to review the situation with the board and compensation committee. But nothing came of it.

Over the next few months, Tamara's colleagues noticed a subtle but significant shift in her demeanor. While she was still professional and hardworking, her usual enthusiasm for tackling complex problems seemed diminished. It was as if something inside her had shut down.

As the company approached a critical development milestone, the impact of Tamara's loss of interest became apparent. Progress slowed, and the team struggled with technical challenges that Tamara would typically have resolved effortlessly.

This sent the CEO into action. Recognizing the potential risk to the company's timeline and valuation, the CEO called a special board meeting. After extensive discussions, they decided to offer Tamara a significant equity refresh grant, along with a seat on the board to ensure her involvement in strategic decisions.

Tamara appreciated the recognition and the effort to address her concerns. After negotiating the terms, she accepted the offer. Over time, her renewed engagement helped the company overcome its technical hurdles and successfully meet its development goals, positioning the company for a strong exit opportunity.

Which is the most correct statement about the CEO's actions?

1. He should not have acquiesced. If everyone demanded more, investors might lose interest in further funding the company.
2. He should have been fair and square from the get-go.
3. The lack of optimal collaboration in the company was a real threat to its success.
4. He is not fit to be a CEO.

The correct answer is 3. CEOs can make mistakes. But this CEO was able to turn things around and make it fair and square after an oversight, or even a deliberate exclusion. Many companies that depend on their human capital—especially start-ups—don't succeed because issues between employees get in the way of effective collaboration. Keeping your eye on the collaborative ball as a CEO is the secret sauce of entrepreneurial success. The comparing brain might have sunk his start-up, but he was able to reverse course by correcting the situation.

# 12

# Secure Priming Therapy: Unearthing Hidden Sparks of Talent

Billions of years ago, evolution introduced an amazing biological "tech" disrupter: molecular diversity. It was a game changer. Molecular diversity allows for small, subtle variations in our molecules, making each of us unique—a one-of-a-kind masterpiece. This uniqueness serves a great evolutionary purpose: It enables life on earth to adapt and thrive in an ever-changing world.

The result is that each of us is like an intricate, multidimensional image assembled of DNA, RNA, proteins, and lipids, all showcasing a dazzling array of molecular complexity. We are like a combination lock with not just three or four digits but tens of thousands. Consider bone marrow transplants as an example: The odds of finding a perfect match range from less than 1 in 10,000 to 1 in 100,000. Even with the lowest estimate of 1 in 10,000, the likelihood of finding three matching donors could be as rare as one in a trillion. In other words, there might only be one or two people in the world who would be a perfect match for you. Fortunately, medical science has advanced enough to allow the use of donors who are not exact matches but are sufficiently similar, so people are able to get this life-saving treatment.

As a neuroscientist, I grapple with the vastness of biological diversity daily. When I'm conducting experiments and analyzing data, biodiversity often feels like a formidable foe, introducing noise into any study. It makes it incredibly difficult, because oftentimes a promising finding disappears in repeated experiments due to too much variance.

That said, what complicates my work as a scientist has transformed my therapeutic approach with patients. Observing biodiversity in the lab has given me an immense appreciation for our unique molecular combinations, which drive a wide array of surprising and interesting talents. I've discovered that helping my patients recognize and cultivate what I've come to call their *hidden sparks of talent* can bring them into greater alignment with their biology, maximize their potential, and foster a greater sense of contentment and security.

I've also come to view attachment styles as biological talents that manifest at certain times. An avoidant attachment style can be advantageous when you need to tackle something alone; anxious attachment style can be beneficial in detecting subtle signals, allowing you to notice important cues before anyone else does; and secure attachment can help you calmly let emotional upsets roll off with relative ease, in turn calming others around you. All attachment styles can be seen as talents bestowed on us by Mother Nature.

Over time in my practice, I've come to notice how innate biological talents manifest in big and small ways in my patients' lives. I've started to actively seek out these talents, and I've found them everywhere I turn. I've also discovered that unearthing these talents with patients is a powerful and important part of helping them become more secure. It doesn't happen overnight, but with persistence and care you rewire the brain toward greater security.

Let me give you an example of how this transpired with one of my patients.

## UNCOVERING HIDDEN SPARKS OF TALENT IN SECURE THERAPY

One of my patients was upset with himself in a session for being indecisive. He kept going back and forth about whether he should stay in his small but inexpensive studio or move to a larger, more expensive apartment, and he just couldn't make up his mind. He hated that he'd been procrastinating over this choice for weeks and saw it as a larger problem, believing he lacked confidence in every area of his life. As he told me this, he frowned and looked down, revealing a mix of dismay and self-doubt.

I pointed out that I did not experience him as a procrastinator and that, in fact, I'd observed him at times acting swiftly and with self-assurance. I reminded him how, a few months prior, his mother had needed to go to respite care because her caregiver was suddenly unavailable and couldn't stay with her. While his brothers were trying to find solutions but came up short, he had, within a few hours, secured a bed in a reputable facility. I mentioned other instances, too, when he had shown similar decisiveness in his private life and at work—whether he was pursuing a new job or ending a relationship.

We discussed how he has an uncanny ability for finding the best deals, the best professionals, the best services. He just has a knack for it, though it takes time and persistence to gather the right information. I reminded him of many examples he had mentioned in passing. For instance, he once found his brother an amazing cruise deal for a fraction of the regular price, something the rest of the family said they never could have pulled off. When his other brother needed home repairs, he located a contractor who charged far less than others and still did impeccable work. At his job this same skill helped him identify under-the-radar opportunities that gave his team a competitive edge. What looked to him like procrastination was, in reality, a hidden spark of talent for thoughtful deliberation—a skill that served him well everywhere he turned. Visibly more at ease, the patient then noted that, in a way, it made sense that he was hesitant to move. It would mean spending significantly more money on rent, and that was money he used to go out in the city, take vacations, and splurge here and there. He was fiscally responsible, and that was a good thing, he reasoned. He said that he now realized that something inside him didn't feel right about moving, and that's why he'd been struggling with the decision. Beyond the money issue, moving itself, and especially in Manhattan, can be overwhelming. He'd been trying to find something decent, but apartments were snatched up quickly, and wherever he showed up there were thirty other people waiting, handing over applications complete with heartfelt essays about why they should be chosen as tenants.

We then explored other reasons why it was important to him to move to a bigger space. But once he was able to free himself from the overbearing self-criticism of his indecisiveness and instead appreciate his inner talent, we could weigh the different aspects of the move from a more secure position.

Showing the patient how he was very good at deliberating about different factors before making decisions is an example of secure priming during a therapy session. In this case, it worked out splendidly. Armed with a better sense of his abilities, he was able to take his time looking for a new place without the usual self-deriding inner commentary; instead, he felt empowered by his newfound confidence. He ultimately found a larger, rent-stabilized apartment in a desirable part of town—and he was able to get it before it even hit the market!

Many people with insecure attachment are overwhelmed by negative thoughts and emotions, and often what they perceive as flaws in their personality are actually hidden sparks of talent, strengths that remain unseen by them or are misunderstood as potential faults or impediments. Unearthing these talents often helps in priming people to become more secure.

## FINDING THE SECURE SILVER LINING

When I trained in psychodynamic psychotherapy, there was a great deal of emphasis on diagnosing and treating the underlying psychopathology that patients presented with. What neurotic or disordered personality trait is the patient exhibiting? Do they manifest narcissistic, borderline, or histrionic characteristics? What about masochistic or sociopathic tendencies? The goal was to understand how to effectively counter these psychopathologies with treatment to facilitate healing.

One of the reasons that I'm drawn toward attachment science is that it's not based on the medical model of fixing pathologies but rather on recognizing normal behavioral traits that are common in everyone. The question then becomes not whether a particular trait or way of looking at things is sick or healthy but rather, is it effective or ineffective? In other words, is it working for you in your life or not, and if not, how can it be changed?

Over the years, while I've remained well-versed in psychodynamic theories, I've naturally gravitated toward a unique mode of treatment I developed that, in a way, is deeply rooted in my own ancestry. My mother was the direct descendent of a well-known eighteenth-century religious scholar who was revered as his congregation's fierce advocate. He always found the silver lining in people's behavior, giving them the benefit of the doubt almost to a fault. Folk stories describe how, even in the face of wrongdoing, he remained lenient and empathetic.

I don't know if it's genetic, but my mother fit that same description, and she, too, followed the tradition of acceptance and leniency. I've come to harness a similar approach with my patients, my students, and the clinicians I supervise—I draw upon my knowledge of neuroscience and psychology for a similarly lenient, accepting perspective. I instinctively listen to people and look for ways I can help them create a secure narrative for themselves so that they can overcome emotional and physical obstacles.

As discussed earlier, Secure Therapy, the method I've created to work with my patients, draws on a field of research called secure priming. Dozens of studies reveal that you can help people become temporarily more secure by exposing them to a short burst of secure cues—for example, by telling them about secure relationships, having them watch movies that depict secure interpersonal interactions, or asking them to read words that convey safety in relationships. In fact, one study found that having couples watch popular relationship movies helped them just as much as being enrolled in structured couples therapy. Even better, studies have found that if you engage in secure priming often and for a longer duration, the security effect lasts longer.

Over time, I've found myself using a clinical form of secure priming in my practice more often. It involves sharing secure priming information drawn from scientific findings, along with anecdotes from movies, plays, and real-life situations, that help patients develop a more secure perspective. In the case of my indecisive patient, secure priming meant showing him how good he was at deliberating about different factors before making decisions. I find that introducing people to secure insights, especially those rooted in our biology and in science, is immensely helpful in instilling long-term security and often leads to dramatic improvements in their lives.

A few weeks after we discussed his conflict about moving, the patient began our session by complaining that he wasn't assertive enough. He wanted to leave his financial adviser, but he was hesitant because he didn't know how to break the news to them. That same week he went to the doctor to talk about his hair loss. The doctor recommended that he apply a cream twice a day, but my patient knew that he wouldn't keep up with the routine and was turned off by the messiness, so he asked for an oral medication instead. The doctor dismissed his request and gave him a prescription for the cream. My patient left feeling frustrated with himself for not being more vocal—and this reinforced his self-image as lacking assertiveness and confidence. Again he was down on himself; even his facial expression revealed feelings of disdain.

## SECURE PRIMING THERAPY

Here, the secure priming intervention took a different route. I told him that before attributing his behavior to a lack of assertiveness, we needed to examine the social backdrop of these interactions. Financial advisers often make it hard for people to leave them. It's part of their job to try to retain as many clients as possible. Like many salespeople, they have ways of making their clients stay, and for anyone who is amicable, it can feel easier to just acquiesce. I shared a story I had read in the paper about a woman who confessed to buying an apartment simply because she didn't know how to say no to the real estate agent. She was visiting Rome from the United States, and the real estate agent who showed her the apartment gave such a hard sell that she found herself buying the place just to avoid turning him down!

The patient's struggle also reminded me of Stanley Milgram's famous experiments measuring obedience in the 1960s, which I shared with him. In one of these experiments, Milgram had his confederate pose as a figure of authority in a room with a study participant. The authority figure then instructed the participant to issue electric shocks to another confederate, who posed as a seemingly unsuspecting person sitting in an adjoining room. The authority figure kept instructing the participant to increase the intensity of the shock (the participant didn't know it was a fake shock). The person being "shocked" cried out, begging them to stop, but more often than not, the participant listened to the authoritative figure and kept shocking the poor fellow. Subsequently, some of the participants, even after being told at the end of the session that they didn't really shock the person, were horribly traumatized by the experience. (In today's world, research ethics committees would never allow such an experiment.)

The famous experiment shows that we can act against our own moral beliefs when an authority figure tells us with determination that we need to do what they say. In another famous experiment, Milgram showed how difficult it is to go against certain social conventions, for instance, cutting ahead in line or refusing a handshake. In this experiment Milgram sent young research assistants to crowded New York City subway cars and told them to ask a seated person, "Excuse me, may I have your seat, please?" To his surprise, most people gave up their seat without a fuss. They couldn't bring themselves to say no.

But that study was revelatory for another reason. An unexpected finding was how hard it was for the research assistants to make such a request. Milgram didn't anticipate how difficult it would be for them. But when they reported back that it was almost impossible to do, he went down to the subway himself and found it excruciatingly difficult to ask people to give up their seat. It took him a few trials before he was able to muster the nerve to do so, and when he did make the request, he found that most of the time he couldn't do it without assuming a sick posture to justify the request, even though his own experimental protocol specifically said not to do that. It was just too hard to ask for the seat with a neutral demeanor. To complete the study, Milgram sent people in pairs, and while it was still hard to do, that made it a little easier.

These classic experiments underscore why, when social forces are at play, it can be so difficult to express your wishes or act on your beliefs (or even act against them!). It might not have anything to do with how assertive you are. The secure lesson is that, when facing a tough social situation, instead of deriding yourself as my patient often did (the common anxious, insecure thing to do), you can recruit others to help you, like the pairs who completed the subway experiment together.

Armed with these insights, my patient began to suffer less self-judgment about his behaviors and was able to call the doctor's office and ask for a change in prescription. He also wrote an email to his financial adviser letting them know that they would be parting ways. But most important, we made progress in challenging his insecure belief system that was telling him he was an indecisive, unassertive procrastinator and, because of that, less of a man.

A few months later, the patient's insecure beliefs resurfaced in the face of a different challenge. He mentioned again that he felt he was too sensitive and not confident or assertive enough; he said that he wished he were "more of a man and less of a wimp." This was in the context of trying to ask women out on dates. He told me that over the years he had experienced an ongoing sense of regret that he didn't listen to his father, who wanted him to go to military boarding school, and instead listened to his mom, who discouraged him from going. He felt that had he gone to military school, he would have toughened up. He often looked at other men with envy, feeling that they were more confident and self-assured than he was and that they aggressively pursued what they wanted, whereas he was soft-spoken and congenial. He wanted what they had. The contrast between his self-perception and his appearance was particularly striking—at six foot two, he was often told that he looked like someone off the cover of a fashion magazine.

We discussed what it meant to him to be manly—and the idea that to be masculine, one needs to be aggressively assertive. To help him become more secure, I pulled out different scientific studies to come to the secure rescue.

It turns out that "survival of the fittest" is not what many people perceive it to be. Like my patient, many people believe that the strongest, most aggressive, and most powerful individuals get all the perks. However, in social species such as African wild dogs, wolves, dolphins, monkeys, and, indeed, humans, where cooperation is key to the well-being of the group, survival of the fittest takes on a different, surprising twist. In many species where males typically leave their troop to find a new home, young, aggressive males are often chased out by impatient females at a much earlier age than usual. Lacking the maturity and experience to survive on their own, many don't make it. In contrast, more amenable males are allowed to remain longer, leaving when they're physically stronger and more experienced—giving them a clear survival advantage.

Agreeableness seems to carry a survival advantage for *Homo sapiens*, too. A prevailing theory for the rise of *Homo sapiens* is that "self-domestication"—reducing our aggressiveness—gave our species the ability to work together, thereby increasing our evolutionary fitness. As I shared this information with my patient, I could see this knowledge seeping in, helping him to reframe his insecure beliefs about himself through this newfound understanding of the important role that being amenable plays in both human evolution and his own life.

## WHEN YOUR BRAIN ADOPTS YOUR SECURE SPIEL

With the information about the aggressive animals and the evolution of our species in mind, my patient adopted the notion that congenial, sensitive men can lead successful, rich, and fulfilling lives. He began to see these traits as a biological gift, something to be celebrated rather than scorned. A few months later, while on vacation, he texted me, referring to the deep-seated feelings of inadequacy, indecisiveness, and lack of confidence he presented with at the start of Secure Therapy:

> Just a little bit ago I was walking down the beach and had a really good feeling come over me, a bit emotional actually. I can tell you more about it on Tuesday. It had to do with a new inner feeling of confidence. And that I know what to do when it really matters.

My patient learned to trust his inner sparks of talent—his ability to navigate the world, gather the right information, and act decisively, even if it meant taking more time and tolerating uncertainty until the right decision emerged. He also came to appreciate his sensitive nature and congeniality. In short, his view of himself became more secure. He's adopted what I've come to call his *secure spiel*.

A secure spiel—meant more in the original connotation of the word *spiel*, which refers to a deeply moving and convincing story you tell, in this case to yourself about who you are—is the ultimate goal of Secure Therapy. By crafting a secure spiel, you essentially form a more balanced narrative about yourself and the world around you.

For my patient, a series of secure priming interventions led to the creation of a secure spiel, which transformed his internal narrative from one of self-criticism and a sense of inadequacy to one that valued his inner sparks of talent. He began to appreciate himself for who he truly was. Each intervention is like a small, secure nudge for the mind—a slight shift in perspective, much like a tiny adjustment at the helm of a massive cruise ship. At first, a small shift may alter the course only slightly, but over time, the ship charts an entirely new course.

Your secure spiel is not only about yourself and your inner sparks. It's a much broader narrative that also identifies others' inner sparks and allows you to view them in a more secure, forgiving way. This secure stance of acceptance can extend to the world around you.

I'm reminded of a patient who would get very upset with her fiancé because, in her mind, he was giving his two adult children much more attention than he gave her. In the course of Secure Therapy, she was able to develop a secure spiel that included the fact that her fiancé was secure and that he could love his children *and* her with all his heart. She had to let go of the idea, shaped by past relationships, that love is a scarce commodity to be competed for or fought over. Secure Therapy helped her see what, for her, due to her anxious attachment style, was hidden in plain sight—that her new partner's secure love knew no bounds. Indeed, with the help of the treatment, she was able to turn her insecure narrative into a secure one and improve her relationship.

## CRAFTING A SECURE SPIEL

Sometimes the process of forming a secure spiel can be implicit—as in the work I described with my patient. Over time, even though we didn't discuss it explicitly, he adopted new secure ideas because of different secure priming interventions and integrated them to create his own spiel. But secure spiels can also be learned more explicitly—meaning you specifically discuss an insecure situation that repeats itself and come up with a secure antidote.

This was the case with Dee Dee. Dee Dee was a capable and skilled therapist. In fact, many of her patients were able to get off medications after working with her, thanks to her hidden spark of talent for seamlessly weaving a wide range of therapeutic approaches into her sessions, matching them to the needs of each patient. But every now and then, she would encounter a patient who objected to her unique integrative approach and became resistant and upset whenever she suggested certain interventions. This always hit a sensitive spot. Harboring her own doubts and insecurities about her training and skills, she would try to accommodate them and bend to their will, but soon discovered that it was futile. They often didn't get better, which only made her feel worse about herself.

In supervision, we explicitly worked on a specific secure spiel: Instead of finding herself trying to acquiesce and go along with what the patient demanded as the treatment progressed, she learned to tell people from the get-go, at the very start of treatment, that she had an integrative approach. She worked by selecting the right tools for them from a number of approaches in which she was well versed. In sessions with me she confidently relayed, "Yes, I gave them my secure spiel and they were on board." Other times she would say, "I told them about how I work, but they wanted something different, so I referred them to someone who better matched what they wanted." Embracing her innate talent and sharing it more effectively with others helped her grow more secure in her work and led to greater contentment in her practice.

Secure Priming Therapy offers a powerful path forward: By unearthing our hidden sparks of talent and weaving them into secure spiels, we transform how we see ourselves and others. These secure narratives become not just stories we tell but lived realities that allow us to navigate life's challenges with greater confidence, compassion, and an appreciation of the unique traits that evolution has gifted each and every one of us.

## HIDDEN SPARK OF TALENT VERSUS IMPEDIMENT INVENTORY

People everywhere have a vast number of hidden sparks of talent. Some sparks are there for the whole world to see. Famous writers and painters, Olympic athletes, and genius mathematicians are a few examples that come to mind. But many talents are hidden in plain sight in the people around you. All you need to do is open your eyes and observe.

In this exercise, you'll explore how a perceived impediment, either your own or that of someone else in your life, might actually reflect a hidden spark of talent—one that simply needs the right environment to thrive.

Instructions:

1. Write down the perceived impediment (either your own or someone else's).
2. Identify the hidden spark of talent that might be behind it.
3. Describe the kind of secure environment that would help this spark of talent flourish.
4. Assign a suitability score from 1 to 10 reflecting how suitable the current environment is for this talent, where 1 is not suitable at all and 10 is the ideal environment for this talent to thrive.

## Example 1: Requiring Constant Input

**Perceived impediment:**
I'm not independent enough. I keep asking for people's opinions and for help deciding what to do—what clothes to wear, when to book a flight, whether to take a vacation this summer. I need input on everything. Why can't I just decide things on my own?

**Hidden spark of talent:**
I'm a very collaborative person, and I feel at my best when I'm working with others who are highly collaborative, too. When we put our minds together to make decisions, we often surface considerations that one of us alone might have missed. I feel more connected this way, and overall, it's worked out well in my life.

**Suitable secure environment:**
A collaborative, team-oriented environment where decisions are made collectively and input is valued, rather than an environment that prizes fierce individualism.

**How suitable is the current environment for this hidden spark of talent?**
*Rate from 1 to 10 (1 = least suitable, 10 = most suitable)*
My husband and kids sometimes get upset when I keep asking for their opinions, and if I had only them, I would give myself a 2, but in the last few years I have made a strong circle of friends, and we're texting and video-calling each other all day long and I can ask them just about anything, even posing in new outfits on video chats and getting their thumbs-up (or down), so I'm giving myself an 8.

## Example 2: My Stubborn Wife

**Perceived impediment:**
My wife is so stubborn and difficult. She's not willing to receive care and doesn't follow her doctor's recommendations. She thinks she knows everything and is unwilling to follow the directions of health-care providers, or anyone else, for that matter.

**Hidden spark of talent:**
Being headstrong and not letting others dictate what you want or need. Being unapologetic about your beliefs and wishes, which is especially challenging for women in our culture.

**Suitable secure environment:**
A physician who is more collaborative than authoritative, who will work with my wife as a team rather than spew instructions.

**How suitable is the current environment for this hidden spark of talent?**
*Rate from 1 to 10 (1 = least suitable, 10 = most suitable)*
Initially my wife had a very authoritative doctor, and they butted heads. My wife refused to take anything she prescribed. Back then it was a 1. She then switched to someone who's patient and friendly, which changed everything. The new doctor was not threatened by my wife's demeanor and was able to win her over. My wife is now taking the medications as prescribed and is doing much better. With this new doctor, it's a 10 out of 10.

## Example 3: The Struggling Corporate Worker

**Perceived impediment:**
My husband is too introverted and sensitive for the corporate world. He used to get overlooked while others got promotions and raises. He felt invisible and unsuccessful.

**Hidden spark of talent:**
He has exceptional gifts for writing and connecting with our children and with the family dog. His sensitivity allows him to tune in to others in ways that more extroverted people often miss.

**Suitable secure environment:**
Writing from home, taking care of the kids part time while I returned to work full time, has been the perfect solution for him. This supports his natural talents rather than expecting him to fit into a traditional corporate mold or gender-based conventions about breadwinning.

**How suitable is the current environment for this hidden spark of talent?**
*Rate from 1 to 10 (1 = least suitable, 10 = most suitable)*
In his corporate job, it was a 2. They completely failed to recognize or make use of his natural abilities, leaving him feeling unsuccessful and invisible. But once he switched to writing from home and looking after the kids, it became an 8. Now our whole family benefits from his natural gifts, and he's written three screenplays to boot.

## Your Turn:

**Perceived impediment:**

**Hidden spark of talent:**

**Suitable secure environment:**

SECURE

**How suitable is the current environment for this hidden spark of talent?**
*Rate from 1 to 10 (1 = least suitable, 10 = most suitable)*

_____

_____

_____

_____

# 13

# Secure Coaching: Learning to Be Secure in Real Time

I used to think that learning to become secure was like learning to ride a bicycle: It takes some getting used to, and initially you may wobble and even fall, but over time you find the right balance. Then I realized that it is much more challenging than learning to ride a bike, because while you're learning secure ways of being, you must also unlearn deep-rooted insecure ones. In a way, it's more like learning how to write with your other hand—it can be so challenging that you just want to use the hand you've always written with. Or like improving your form when you swim, adjusting your posture to ward off back pain, or correcting your pronunciation and enunciation. These kinds of shifts ask you to learn something new while also letting go of old habits that are entrenched in your brain.

From a neuroscience perspective, relearning requires two processes—unlearning something you already know and learning something new to replace it. Studies show that unlearning (which is a form of forgetting) is an active molecular process that involves the deconstruction of the synapse that connects two neurons, so that their connection is not as tight.

Active learning engages the opposite pattern, strengthening and building more scaffolding in certain synapses so that the connections are tighter. It's believed that the structure of our synapses holds most of our memories, and these memories—or in the case of secure priming, learned emotional lessons—are forever pulled between the yin and the yang of learning and forgetting. This constant interplay shapes a neuronal system that's exquisitely sensitive to our environment in a phenomenon called neuroplasticity.

Each experience we have can either strengthen or weaken the connections between specific synapses, thereby reinforcing or diminishing certain neuronal networks. Our surroundings are constantly at play, actively shaping the brain and who we are.

Given all this, becoming secure may seem like an impossible double whammy, requiring you to do away with the old while trying out the new. You can achieve that by immersing yourself in the right SIMIs, the seemingly insignificant minor interactions of everyday life. When you engage in secure SIMIs and phase out insecure ones, you actively reshape your environment to boost your brain's secure neuronal networks. In other words, you actually get to reshape your synapses and your brain! In this way, you can leave behind the old insecurities and embrace a new, secure way to view the world.

This was the case with Tammy, whose story I told in chapter 8. Despite growing up in an insecure household and having many insecure relationships, over time she was able to switch out most of the insecure SIMIs in her life for secure ones, and with that, her mind opened up to the world. She took painting lessons, went to shows, visited museums, became a certified cycling instructor, and traveled the world. In short, she developed a full, secure life for herself and never looked back.

SECURE COACHING: LEARNING TO BE SECURE IN REAL TIME

## REAL-TIME SECURE COACHING INTERVENTIONS

Real-time interventions can be enormously valuable to break free of insecure habits. In fact, they often serve as a bridge between insight and action—helping clients shift out of old patterns as they occur rather than reflecting on them in session. This is where Secure Coaching becomes especially helpful. While Secure Therapy helps clients reexamine deep-rooted beliefs and behaviors within the structure of the therapeutic hour, Secure Coaching focuses on helping clients improve with specific, actionable interventions that happen in real time. In secure treatment, the two modalities are always used together to support the process of becoming more secure. Here's an example that illustrates the impact of real-time Secure Coaching.

A patient presented with ongoing frustration and upsets in his marriage. He and his wife fought frequently, hurling insults that went straight for the jugular—using intimate knowledge of vulnerable moments to hurt each other. In our sessions I focused on helping him deal with conflict in a more secure way, encouraging him to understand his wife's perspective and remember that he still loved her even while he was upset. However, much of what we discussed in sessions would go out the window when they fought. He would resort to his old habit of lashing out, she would respond in kind, and both would then retreat to their corner of the house, licking their emotional wounds.

I encouraged my patient to text me in real time when things started up between them, but for several months he did not. Because of his insecure attachment style, he was not used to asking for help. Finally, one evening he texted the following: "She is such a piece of work. She just ignores me on purpose. Who the fuck does she think she is? I'm not going to just sit there and let her run me over emotionally."

I immediately texted back and reminded him that she got that way when she felt hurt, overlooked, or let down by him, that it was an instinct she had—she just recoiled with very little control over it. I also reminded him of the times when she'd stood by him, like the previous winter when he'd needed multiple surgeries after he'd had a bike accident. She was there by his side, supporting him in the most loving, thoughtful way. I pointed out the hardships in her own life: Her father had died of lymphoma when she was very young. Her mother had remarried, and her stepfather had abused her. So when she got upset and felt slighted, she clammed up. She didn't mean to, and she regretted it later.

It took a few more rounds of texts, but my patient was able to calm down. "Yes, you're right," he texted. "I guess I don't have to take it to heart so much. She's upset with me, and it will pass. We both didn't have it easy growing up, and we both have to deal with two challenging kids. Truth be told, we're doing a pretty good job under the circumstances." He was able to approach her calmly and say, "I know I upset you and that's why you're withdrawing, and that saddens me. Can we please make up? I really apologize, I didn't mean to hurt you, that's the last thing I'd ever want. Can we hug?"

To his surprise, she got up and they hugged, defusing the tension. Not only was the potential escalation of the argument thwarted, but they also learned a new secure coping skill.

With relatively little effort, the patient was able to see things more securely at the onset of what could have been a very difficult argument and shift his behavior, leading to a radically different outcome. I encouraged him to reach out to me early on during future arguments, which he did, and we managed to divert several potential emotional blowouts. Eventually, his wife began to clam up less during upsets, which greatly helped the patient, whose main trigger was being stillfaced by her.

I've found Secure Coaching and its real-time interventions to be one of the most effective ways to help people move toward security. Just reaching out for help *while* you're distressed—not hours or days later—is itself a secure behavior. Studies show that that's a secure hallmark—

knowing to recruit others to help you in time of need. It's a key skill that people with secure attachment naturally use, and one that others can actively learn.

Once someone reaches out, what happens next matters just as much. A secure person—whether a therapist, coach, or trusted friend—can step in with a grounded, secure perspective, helping to interrupt the cycle of hurt and reactivity as it's unfolding. This not only prevents further emotional harm; it also models a secure way of responding: with calm, care, and clarity.

Over time, you begin to build a network of secure people you can rely on, and you start to internalize the secure mindset for yourself. This is one of the main goals of Secure Therapy and Secure Coaching.

### USING AI FOR YOUR REAL-TIME SECURE INTERVENTIONS

If you are having a challenging interaction with another person, you can use the following prompts to help AI assist you in finding a more secure stance. Simply type up the basic scenario; for example, "My friend promised to go to a basketball game with me and canceled at the last minute." Or you can paste an email or a text you received from someone that you find offensive or upsetting. If you ask AI questions like the ones listed below, it will help you craft a secure response. Even if you don't use the response with the person, it can help you form a secure spiel about what happened. Try these:

- How can I respond to this kindly?
- Can you give me their potential point of view?
- How can I find a way not to upset them?
- What should I be grateful for in regards to this person?
- How can I answer this in a conciliatory way?

- How can I de-escalate the situation?
- Help me find a way to be less upset about this situation.

If AI gives you an answer that isn't helpful, don't give up. Instead, explain why it's not helpful and keep asking for what you need. Treat it like a conversation—it will learn from your feedback and respond more effectively over time. Let it know what hasn't worked and what *has* worked for you in the past. With a little practice, it can become an incredibly helpful and secure companion for navigating tough situations.

That said, AI cannot replace the human support in your life. Make sure you've also identified people you trust to be your secure base. You can even ask them to help you assess whether what the AI is recommending is grounded.

## RULES OF SECURE ENGAGEMENT

When it comes to handling conflict in close relationships, emotional regulation often breaks down right when it's needed most. That's because staying calm in the face of another person's distress is one of the hardest things to do—especially when your own emotions are flaring up, too. To help navigate these moments, I often teach two simple but powerful rules that can make a real difference.

1. *The Only One Person Is Allowed to Be Upset at a Time Rule.* The first person who gets upset, it's their turn, and it's your responsibility to help them calm down and defuse the situation. The reason is simple: From the point of view of the social brain, a person's designated role in a secure relationship is to help regulate affect and emotions, not stir them up. After the person calms down—but not at the same time—you can take your turn and be upset. Otherwise, if you both get upset, you're like two cats who climb up a tree and can't come down, hissing and clawing at each other, stuck in emotional limbo. In my practice, a

couple might start to get upset, and one person will say, "Excuse me, we're now both upset, but that's against the rules. I was upset first, so it's my turn. You have to help me feel better." More often than not, they burst out laughing. This rule applies to all close relationships, not just romantic ones. It holds true for friends, siblings, parents, children, and others.

2. *The Mea Culpa Rule* (or, "It's my fault"). If rule number one failed and you both find yourself upset, don't panic. This is very common. When we're connected to someone, a single emotional field forms between us, and one person's upset naturally ripples through it. Of course you'll feel it. The real question is: Will you let it topple you?

   Think about it this way: You're both responsible for failing to maintain each other's emotional equilibrium. Now the two of you need to apologize. The apology isn't about who was right or wrong—it's about recognizing that you were both unsuccessful in a more important mission: helping each other stay calm. It has to be sincere and show true awareness of where you went wrong. For example: "I'm really sorry that I upset you and wasn't able to make it better. I can be so thoughtless sometimes, even a jerk. I should have helped you feel better. I was selfishly focused on my own self-righteous, sanctimonious point of view."

   Both sides need to offer this kind of heartfelt, self-aware apology—a modern-day mea culpa, if you will. This helps defuse the emotional divide between two angry people.

## MASTERING THE SECURE WAY

Why is it that secure people can say no relatively easily, and without the ensuing drama, and how can Secure Coaching help?

From an attachment perspective, terms like *people-pleasing*, *boundary setting*, and *codependence* often lead people astray in their efforts to become more secure, and they all share a common myth—that greater contentment is achieved by protecting our individual well-being. It's true but misleading—because our individual well-being is inextricably tied to that of the people around us. Our culture tends to promote individuality and independence as the path to growth. But from our social brain's perspective, that's not the direct solution. Hyperconnectedness is key to both physical and mental wellness. The real issue then becomes, hyperconnected to whom?

When we're in a secure relationship, we can "please" others freely—do things for them—because we trust they'll do the same for us. And if we can't, we feel okay saying no, without worrying it'll upset them. This is especially true if the other person scores high on the Collaborative Assessment Scale (presented in chapter 11)—the back-and-forth of what we do for them and what they do for us just works well with these individuals.

People think that secures are amazing at navigating relationships, and they are, but the irony is that their ease comes as much from a less sensitive threat radar as from social skill. Unlike anxious attachers, who often have remarkable perceptual acuity, secure people's perceptual systems tend to be "duller." They simply don't pick up on as many subtle cues that might suggest threat or rejection. That's why they can so easily say, "Sorry, I can't," without even registering that it might upset someone. And often, because they say it so simply and sincerely, it doesn't. In contrast, when insecure people say no, they often become anxiously apologetic (if anxious) or withdrawn (if avoidant)—and inadvertently create relationship strife.

Because secures get less riled up during disagreements—since they don't register them as threats—they can communicate more clearly, avoid lashing out, and help iron things out more smoothly. Thanks to their "duller" senses, they don't see arguments as the end of the world, just a hiccup that will pass. And with that attitude, things often end up repairing themselves.

I've watched with fascination a trend on social media where people prank their partners by pretending to shoot a video about something else

## SECURE COACHING: LEARNING TO BE SECURE IN REAL TIME

and then casually referring to "me and my current boyfriend/girlfriend" or "my current husband/wife." You see all kinds of reactions. Some partners blow up or withdraw, clearly distressed—"What do you mean 'current'?" they say with great dismay. "Are you replacing me? Why would you say that?" Some even utter expletives. But others laugh—or don't even register it as anything unusual. You can see, in real time, how not picking up on things—in this case, things that were done deliberately to rattle you—can make relationships so much easier.

When your perceptual system isn't so good at picking up potential threats, day-to-day interactions are easier. You can deal with things as they come up quietly, with little effort, simply because there's no alarm blaring in the background—no "They mistreated me" or "They're not fair" or "They want too much." But for many insecurely attached people, that alarm goes off easily and frequently, especially in non-CARRP situations. It makes many interactions feel extra fraught, because you're left to manage relationships with insecure chatter in your head.

That's why real-time Secure Coaching interventions can be so powerful. You get someone who doesn't have the constant internal alarm to offer a grounded, secure perspective. That perspective is enough to shut the alarm off, even if temporarily, allowing you to respond securely. That shift, in the moment, can interrupt vicious cycles as they occur and make a huge difference in securing relationships.

---

Real-time secure interventions are immensely helpful for undoing insecure behaviors as they arise. But many of us also carry long-standing insecure patterns that run quietly in the background, shaping our thoughts, feelings, and choices in ways that hold us back. In addition to building a secure support network, it's equally important to recognize and confront these patterns directly.

The idea is this: Where there is ongoing, underlying insecurity, let there be a secure way of relating—to yourself and to the world.

The next section outlines some of the most common insecure thought patterns—and the secure counterparts that can replace them.

## ENHANCING YOUR SECURE STANCE BY AVOIDING THESE PITFALLS

There are several common pitfalls that can stand in the way of becoming more secure. These pitfalls often result in an insecure spiel and achieve the opposite of what you want, reinforcing insecure neuronal networks rather than forging new, secure ones. Minding these insecure pitfalls will help you change the habitual insecure ways of thinking that you unconsciously fall into without even noticing.

It's a bit like correcting your posture. At first it feels unnatural, even tiring, because your body is so used to slouching. But with awareness and repetition, your muscles adjust, and over time, standing tall starts to feel like second nature.

The pitfalls are organized into three main groups: (A) Overlooking or Misinterpreting Sparks of Talent; (B) Ignoring Biological Needs and Environmental Fit; and (C) Self-Defeating, Insecure Mental Patterns.

### Group A: Overlooking or Misinterpreting Sparks of Talent

**PITFALL 1:** Not respecting your inner calling—ignoring it in favor of something else.

**INSTEAD:** Be attuned to your sparks of talent.

Sometimes people pressure themselves based on external influences—like societal expectations or conventions about what is more desirable or good for them—rather than listening to their inner calling. They think they

# SECURE COACHING: LEARNING TO BE SECURE IN REAL TIME

should be a lawyer because it's expected of them, but they hate arguing and confrontation. Or they think it would be really cool to be an artist—everyone in their family is one—but they actually excel in gymnastics, even though no one in their family is the least bit athletically inclined.

However, when you're in alignment with your inner spark of talent, you gain an immediate secure boost—it's easier for you to function in the world from a more secure stance because you're anchored in your biological truth. Embracing your natural talents can be profoundly stabilizing. It builds self-esteem and creates a sense of inner congruence—a key component of secure functioning.

**PITFALL 2:** Overlooking people's sparks of talent or, worse, seeing these sparks as impediments.

**INSTEAD:** See sparks of talent in people all around you and discover that behind perceived impediments may lie marvels of talent.

I often have to remind people that it's unwise to disregard sparks of talent or, worse, see them as impediments. For instance, imagine you're frustrated with your partner for spending long hours mentoring others at work, because this takes time away from your relationship. But when you do ask for their help or support, they show up fully and are always thoughtful, generous, and committed. If someone's inner spark of talent is a deep commitment to helping others, it's likely to show up in every part of their life. You can't selectively enjoy it, appreciating their dedication and generosity when it's directed at you while resenting it when it benefits others.

Focusing on those sparks can help you see others—and yourself—through a more secure lens.

In general, being overly critical of others instead of unearthing their hidden sparks of talent can get in the way of your secure mindset. Focusing on those sparks can shift how you see people—and the world around you!

## Group B: Ignoring Biological Needs and Environmental Fit

**PITFALL 3:** Not shying away from an environment that doesn't suit your biology.

**INSTEAD:** Be respectful of your biological limitations.

One big trap that people fall into is setting up an environment that's at odds with their biology. As discussed in part 2, if you tend toward an anxious attachment style and surround yourself with non-CARRP people, or, on the flip side, if you have more of an avoidant style but others around you want the kind of closeness that makes you want to flee, it will be very hard to make it work. In general, even beyond attachment styles, expecting your biology to adapt to an environment that isn't suitable for you can be extremely challenging.

I'm reminded of a patient who was highly sensitive to noise. He lived with his spouse in a large one-bedroom facing a busy avenue on the Upper West Side in Manhattan. On garbage day, he'd be jolted awake at ungodly hours by the clanging and banging of garbage trucks. Across the street was a major supermarket, so he constantly heard trucks idling for hours and beeping as they backed up. Add to that people yelling drunkenly at night and the city's nonstop hum, and he really suffered. He was irritable and snappy and complained all the time. His spouse, meanwhile, barely noticed. He slept through everything and could tune out the noise without much effort.

After a few years of misery, my patient finally hit his limit. He found another apartment in the building, one that faced the inner courtyard in the back. Even though it was smaller and more expensive, he badgered his partner to move. His partner objected: "That's crazy—to move to a smaller apartment and pay more money. The noise isn't so bad. Honestly, you just have to let it go." They fought about it several times until his partner finally acquiesced.

## SECURE COACHING: LEARNING TO BE SECURE IN REAL TIME

Now, several years later, his partner says it's the best decision they ever made. It's made a world of difference in their lives and their relationship. My patient is a changed person: calmer, sweeter, and far more grounded. "It was a great move on your part," his partner jokes with his dorky humor. "Pun intended, pun intended," he always adds. My patient says he can't help but roll his eyes, and then they both laugh; it's become one of their recurrent private jokes.

Remember, if you happen to have an orchid biological sensitivity, like sensitivity to noise, trying to tough it out doesn't usually work. So many orchids try to force themselves to be dandelions. Then, when reality hits, they suffer. "Why can't I be less sensitive? I shouldn't take this to heart," they often think to themselves. But ignoring or, even worse, butting heads with your biology isn't going to change it. It just makes coping harder. It also misses something crucial about orchids—when you get your biological needs met, you can then realize your full potential and end up outperforming dandelions!

**PITFALL 4:** Not seeking out the best environment to maximize your inner sparks of talent.

**INSTEAD:** Actively find a favorable habitat.

Avoiding an unfavorable environment is one thing, but actively seeking out an ideal setting where your talents can flourish can give you a significant advantage. For instance, imagine you excel in the technical aspects of your job when working independently, but your current role happens to involve managing many people. Pursuing an environment that allows your natural abilities to shine—such as a job in which you can focus on a technical challenge without having to manage many people—can enhance your skills, greatly increase your productivity, and boost your morale.

## Group C: Self-Defeating, Insecure Mental Patterns

**PITFALL 5:** Berating yourself.

**INSTEAD:** Practice acceptance and look for ways to improve your situation.

One of my patients often became worked up while looking for a parking spot on the Upper West Side in Manhattan. He would berate himself: "I'm the unluckiest person in the world. I never catch a break. Why do bad things always happen to me?" The more blocks he circled, the more agitated he became. By the time he finally found a spot, he'd exhausted himself with negative thoughts, unable to recognize the toll his insecure chatter was taking on his health and happiness.

Parking in Manhattan is notoriously a nightmare. There's nothing personal about it, and it requires emotional resilience. You can have someone else park for you, sign up for a parking garage, or even get rid of your car. But subjecting yourself to ongoing insecure self-criticism is very damaging. Many people fall into this trap when things don't go their way. It all comes down to the same pitfall: forgetting that we all face hardships, and we all make mistakes. Once you accept this, you can approach difficult situations from a more secure stance.

**PITFALL 6:** Imagining a perfect alternate universe that makes you feel ungrateful and miserable in this one.

**INSTEAD:** Adopt the "life is a mixed bag" paradigm.

Every choice we make in life comes with pros and cons, and as with most things, the result is a mixed bag: There are good and bad aspects to each situation. That said, it's not worth wasting your time pining for an alternate life that might have been. For example, a psychiatrist once confided that he sometimes regretted not pursuing his early dream of becoming a geologist. He loved nature and was fascinated by the earth's history. He

## SECURE COACHING: LEARNING TO BE SECURE IN REAL TIME

imagined a life spent exploring remote landscapes, making exciting discoveries, and being more adventurous. Despite having a successful career making a real difference in people's lives, he couldn't shake the feeling that he had missed his true calling. But the reality is that the life of an academic geologist comes with its own challenges—long periods away from home, working in harsh and sometimes dangerous environments, and dealing with the uncertainty of research funding. Had he chosen that path, he might have faced isolation, physical hardship, and frustration over the slow progress of research. It's easy to romanticize an alternate path, but every choice comes with its own set of challenges. Imagining that a different life would have been better for you only makes you less satisfied with the life you have now.

Sometimes you get to witness firsthand how this plays out in real life. A patient of mine who's a cybersecurity wizard often fantasized about becoming a bartender. The more he thought about the carefree work of bartending, the less happy he became with his current job—constantly trying to outsmart conniving people with malicious intent over the internet. Drawn in by his fantasy, he started working part time in his tech job and enrolled in bartending school. But reality hit fast when he got his first bartending gig and discovered the other side of the job—schlepping boxes of bottles from the basement, washing a mountain of dishes every night, dealing with rowdy crowds, and enduring patrons' endless drunkalogues, which got old real fast.

While he loved learning to make different cocktails in bartending school, he was also relieved to return to his cybersecurity work with a newfound appreciation for his talents and position. He suddenly saw his cybersecurity work in a different light—he was the defender of the cyberuniverse. His job was to keep people safe and secure, even if they didn't know it. This experience taught him that while the bartender life seemed appealing in theory, it was an unrealistic fantasy that made him less appreciative of his work. It sure wasn't the glamorous, carefree existence he had envisioned.

His trying—and failing at—a new line of work while in Secure Therapy gave us an opportunity to use the "setback" to help reset his inner narrative to a more secure one. Before, he was constantly criticizing his job, feeling it lacked meaning. But after this experience, he discovered a newfound sense of purpose in the very job he had once dismissed. It shifted his stance entirely, allowing him to approach his work from a more secure place—and completely changed how he experienced it.

**PITFALL 7:** Comparing and despairing—letting your comparing neurocircuitry go rogue by assuming that other people are happier because they have things you don't have.

**INSTEAD:** Resist letting people's external circumstances—relationships, possessions, beauty—push you to conclude they're happier than you and to feel bad about yourself as a result. Focus on what brings you fulfillment, and use the tools in this book to create a secure, supportive environment.

In the 1950s, the advent of television coincided with a surprising increase in depression and anxiety among housewives in the United States. The cause wasn't immediately clear, but a potential link soon came into focus: commercials. Women across the country were watching commercials with beautiful actresses "cleaning" the bathroom while singing and smiling, and thought to themselves, "What's wrong with my life? How come I don't feel like breaking into a song and a dance while wearing perfect makeup and a fabulous dress when I'm cleaning my house?" It made a whole generation of women feel that there was something wrong with them until, over time, people learned to see commercials for what they are—staged portrayals of an idealized life.

In today's social media–saturated world, the comparison game has only intensified. Unlike commercials, which most of us now recognize as staged and artificial, social media blurs the line. It doesn't just show actors—it shows *people we know.* That makes it much harder for the brain to label an event highlighted on social media as fantasy. When you see

## SECURE COACHING: LEARNING TO BE SECURE IN REAL TIME

your friends dining without you or off on a dreamy vacation you weren't invited to, it doesn't feel like a performance—it feels personal. But the truth is, what you're seeing is still a curated slice of life, carefully filtered and cropped. It's not real life, either—it just *feels* more real, and that's what makes it so tricky.

A patient of mine told me about a couple he knows who, on social media, seemed like they had the perfect relationship: They used "#MyBabe" to chronicle their travels around the world and often professed their love for each other in public posts. But behind the scenes, they fought constantly. The only times they got along were when they were distracted by one of their fabulous trips—and even then, it was far from perfect. They literally needed to be on the move so as not to be at each other's throats. Yet you wouldn't know it from their social media, which captured a seemingly endless stream of smiles, kisses, and sunsets in exotic places.

Letting your comparing neurocircuitry (described in chapter 11)—which is exquisitely tuned to the haves and have-nots—lead you to believe that external things might make you happy is one of the gravest mistakes you can make. And left unchecked, it can be hard to rein in. As you now know, it's in the very nature of that neurocircuitry to compare. But you can rise above it. You don't have to let it deflate you or chip away at your well-being. Instead, focus on building a hyperconnected, secure environment for yourself—as outlined in chapters 2 and 3—to strengthen your self-esteem and deepen your sense of meaning in life.

A now-famous Harvard longitudinal study that began in 1938 followed 724 men from all walks of life—rich and poor, university professors and high school dropouts—for more than 80 years (and continues to follow 90 of the original participants as well as the offspring of the original 724, both men and women). It found that the quality of their close relationships was by far the biggest determinant of their continued well-being, both physical and mental. And the Harvard study is not alone; several other studies have shown the same thing. If you stop to think about it, this measure of happiness—meaningful, secure ties with others—can't be captured and posted online. Secure SIMIs with supportive CARRP people who convey caring, loving attitudes can occur in small and subtle ways day in and day out. They are the elixir of our social soul.

When you find yourself comparing and despairing over external things, catch yourself for a moment and instead, with a sense of gratitude, think about the secure relationships in your life and the road you're paving toward your secure village. Though being secure isn't easily captured on camera and posted on social media, it is a real, identifiable, and lasting path to long-term life satisfaction. Think of it as a major life achievement, the holy grail of human happiness, which fame, money, and social stature can't buy.

## Summary of the things that stand in your way of becoming more secure

### The two rules of secure engagement

Rule 1: The Only One Person Is Allowed to Be Upset at a Time Rule
Rule 2: The Mea Culpa ("It's my fault") Rule

### Insecure Pitfalls Table

| GROUP A: OVERLOOKING OR MISINTERPRETING SPARKS OF TALENT | GROUP B: IGNORING BIOLOGICAL NEEDS AND ENVIRONMENTAL FIT | GROUP C: SELF-DEFEATING, INSECURE MENTAL PATTERNS |
|---|---|---|
| **PITFALL 1:** Not respecting your inner calling—ignoring it in favor of something else. **INSTEAD:** Be attuned to your sparks of talent. | **PITFALL 3:** Not shying away from an environment that doesn't suit your biology. **INSTEAD:** Be respectful of your biological limitations. | **PITFALL 5:** Berating yourself. **INSTEAD:** Practice acceptance and look for ways to improve your situation. |

| GROUP A: OVERLOOKING OR MISINTERPRETING SPARKS OF TALENT | GROUP B: IGNORING BIOLOGICAL NEEDS AND ENVIRONMENTAL FIT | GROUP C: SELF-DEFEATING, INSECURE MENTAL PATTERNS |
|---|---|---|
| PITFALL 2: Overlooking people's sparks of talent or, worse, seeing these sparks as impediments.<br><br>INSTEAD: See sparks of talent in people all around you and discover that behind perceived impediments may lie marvels of talent. | PITFALL 4: Not seeking out the best environment to maximize your inner sparks of talent.<br><br>INSTEAD: Actively find a favorable habitat. | PITFALL 6: Imagining a perfect alternate universe that makes you feel ungrateful and miserable in this one.<br><br>INSTEAD: Adopt the "life is a mixed bag" paradigm. |
|  |  | PITFALL 7: Comparing and despairing—letting your comparing neurocircuitry go rogue by assuming that other people are happier because they have things you don't have.<br><br>INSTEAD: Resist letting people's external circumstances—relationships, possessions, beauty—push you to conclude they're happier than you and to feel bad about yourself as a result. Focus on what brings you fulfillment, and use the tools in this book to create a secure, supportive environment. |

## A SECURE COACHING WORKSHOP

### Securing Sylvia

Mark's business partner constantly belittled him in front of the whole office, yet Mark always responded with patience and respect. That was his way with everyone, including his wife, Sylvia, who often chastised him with snide remarks and neglected her share of the household chores. Mark would step up and take care of everything, rarely confronting her for being mean or not pulling her weight.

Sylvia was also often treated badly by Mark's business partner, but Mark didn't really stand up for her. For a long time, Sylvia resented Mark for that. When, in Secure Therapy, she realized that his lack of assertiveness with his partner wasn't weakness but rather a hidden spark of talent, patience, and tolerance, it transformed how she viewed the situation, and him. She felt fortunate that she had such a tolerant partner, knowing full well she was a hard person to get along with.

However, her newly found appreciation of her husband didn't change the fact that whenever they got together with Mark's business partner, she came home close to tears. Mark kept telling her that she shouldn't let it bother her, and she tried not to pay attention to his partner's demeaning remarks. After all, he was just as mean to Mark, and Mark didn't care. But no matter how hard she tried, the man's words always managed to get under her skin.

Which pitfall did Sylvia overcome to transform her relationship with Mark?

1. Overlooking people's sparks of talent or, worse, seeing these sparks as impediments.
2. Not creating an environment that is suitable for your inner calling.

# SECURE COACHING: LEARNING TO BE SECURE IN REAL TIME

3. Not having the right social surroundings to help you nurture your sparks of talent.

4. Not shying away from a physical environment that doesn't suit your biology (trying to be a dandelion when you're an orchid).

5. Not respecting your inner calling.

The correct answer is 1, overlooking people's sparks of talent or, worse, seeing these sparks as impediments. Once Sylvia was able to see Mark's behavior for what it was—a hidden spark of talent—she was able to let go of her ongoing resentment, appreciate him more, and become more secure in their relationship.

Even though Sylvia was able to become more secure in her relationship with Mark, she still reacts insecurely with his business partner.

Which pitfall provides a hint toward the right course of action in terms of what Sylvia needs to do to become more secure?

1. Berating yourself.

2. Not respecting your inner calling.

3. Viewing people's hidden sparks of talent as an impediment.

4. Not shying away from an environment that doesn't suit your biology.

5. Imagining a perfect alternate universe that makes you feel ungrateful and miserable in this one.

The correct answer is 4. If you expose yourself to an onslaught of insecure SIMIs again and again, it will affect your brain in a detrimental way. Therefore, if the situation can't be resolved in a way that prevents Sylvia from being hurt by Mark's business partner, it would be better for her to refrain from joining Mark when he meets with him and instead seek out a more secure social alternative. We might feel obligated to attend unfavorable social events because of societal expectations, but exposing yourself to insecure SIMIs is a surefire way to prolong an insecure vicious cycle of recurrent hurts. Sometimes the secure thing to do is not to force yourself into an unfavorable situation but to find an alternative secure social event to attend instead, one that will reinforce your new secure ways rather than derail them.

## The "Pushover" Therapist

Dee Dee, the supervisee featured in chapter 12 who constructed her secure spiel with her patients, usually gives herself freely to them. They can text and call between sessions and she makes it a point to be available to them almost 24/7. She has worked with treatment resistant patients and helped them improve dramatically where other therapists failed. However, Dee Dee now has a patient who's essentially taken over her life. She calls constantly, demanding to talk at all hours, and when Dee Dee isn't immediately available, she launches into a tirade, cursing and sending a barrage of obscene, angry texts.

In our supervision session, Dee Dee confessed that she felt she needed to overhaul the way she was doing therapy. She'd been too permissive, too accommodating, and she believed all that needed to change. She went on to recount her relationship with her mother growing up. She said she used to take in a constant stream of criticism and ill will from her, and this pattern is now repeating itself in her work with patients. She explained that she always felt bad for her mother because her father was a notorious womanizer who had countless affairs. He didn't even bother to conceal it, and Dee Dee could see how much it hurt her mother and how she suffered in the marriage. That was why Dee Dee tolerated her behavior and tried to show her consideration and love. Her heart went out to her.

In another supervision session, Dee Dee again expressed that she was feeling overwhelmed by the same patient, who was calling and texting her at all hours of the night. She had also had a midnight session with a differ-

## SECURE COACHING: LEARNING TO BE SECURE IN REAL TIME

ent patient because that was the only time the patient was able to get away from her abusive husband, and Dee Dee was concerned for her safety. She criticized herself for being too tolerant and accepting, again emphasizing that she believed it all stemmed from her inability to stand up to her mother during her childhood. She was a pushover then, and now her patients were treating her exactly as her mother did.

Which is the most correct statement?

Dee Dee...

1. Needs to overhaul the way she conducts therapy, imposing stricter boundaries in her work with her patients.
2. Is not fit to be a therapist because she fails to maintain the structure and boundaries of therapy, i.e., the therapeutic frame.
3. Needs help with some of these patients she finds difficult to manage.
4. Needs to explore in her own therapy her childhood trauma, which is interfering with her work.

The most correct answer is 3.

Dee Dee does not need to completely overhaul the way she conducts treatment. She's helped so many patients, some of whom were not able to get better for decades despite trying many different treatments. Clearly, Dee Dee is doing many things right, and her treatment style, which is all-encompassing and almost like surrogate parenting, is unparalleled. However, some patients are not the best match for the kind of care she provides, and while exploring her childhood experiences with her mother in treatment can be helpful, the most immediate and effective way to address the problem is to get help managing this specific patient.

In supervision, we were able to see that Dee Dee had an extraordinary empathic caregiving ability, which helped her show up for her patients in abundance. This was one of the reasons she was such a successful therapist. Her ability was already evident when she was a child. She wasn't a "pushover" with her mother. She could sense that her mother was suffering, and she wanted to be there for her and help her because she loved her. Her love simply overlooked her mother's mean behavior; she could see beyond it.

We discussed how there's also a biological basis for this amazing empathic caregiving. Research has found that animals who are exceptional mothers and caregivers have higher levels of oxytocin receptors in the reward areas of their brains—making caregiving not a sign of defeat but a rewarding and gratifying talent they can bring to the world around them.

That being said, with certain patients who took over her life, Dee Dee needed help with several real-time secure interventions to manage the onslaught of calls and texts as they unfolded and help her respond to the patient in the moment. She also needed to recognize that sometimes patients required more than she could provide, and by trying to go it alone, she was stalling their recovery. In these cases, she referred them to a higher level of care where they could be treated by a team of clinicians with more resources.

Referring out wasn't easy. It often triggered a wave of anxiety in Dee Dee—she worried how the patient might react, whether she'd be seen as abandoning them, or if the patient would spiral. We worked together to craft a secure spiel she could use in those moments—one that emphasized care, not rejection.

## Loren's True Calling

Loren is in her late thirties and feels that she has wasted her life because she hasn't pursued a career or developed any specific skills. Everyone around her has an advanced graduate degree, while she stopped with a bachelor's. Yet when you look at her life more closely, it's clear that she has a brilliant head for business and is the major intellectual force behind the family company she started with her husband. She is also creative and insightful, constantly learning new things, and her friends regularly turn to her for advice on how to navigate challenges in their lives.

SECURE COACHING: LEARNING TO BE SECURE IN REAL TIME

What is Loren's hidden talent?

1. Self-awareness in acknowledging her educational deficits
2. Her innate curiosity and desire to learn
3. A brilliant head for business
4. A creative problem solver

The correct answers are 2, 3, and 4. Loren is a creative problem solver with a unique view of the world. She's also exceptionally good at guiding and helping people to reach their full potential, a natural healer and caregiver who empowers everyone around her to flourish. Her friends gravitate toward her knowledge and skills, which have also played a major role in the success of the family business. But because she never earned an advanced degree, Loren feels like she missed her calling. In reality, she's been true to her calling all along.

Which pitfall does Loren need to overcome to become more secure?

1. Overlooking your sparks of talent or, worse, seeing them as impediments.
2. Not creating a physical environment that is suitable for your inner calling.
3. Not having the right social surroundings to help you nurture your sparks of talent.
4. Trying to be a dandelion when you're an orchid.
5. Missing one's calling—imagining a perfect alternate universe that makes you feel ungrateful and miserable in this one.

The correct answers are 1 and 5. Loren doesn't recognize that she has been using her talents to better herself and mentor others around her all along. And her talents have given her a rich and rewarding life running a successful family business and maintaining strong relationships with her friends and family. Getting an advanced degree doesn't guarantee a fulfilling life. In fact, many people struggle during graduate school, and some even regret pursuing it. Loren is a curious person who has continued to learn throughout her life in various ways, and this has been greatly fulfilling for her, even without a degree attached to it.

## Not Making It in the Big League

A divorced finance executive in his late forties shared in therapy that he felt like a failure because of the way his career had turned out. He had always been a salary man, working in large institutions while others in his field took the plunge and started their own venture capital firms, making hundreds of millions, even billions of dollars. "I played it safe, stayed at a salary position, and missed out on becoming much wealthier by taking a risk and opening my own firm, the way many of my friends and colleagues who became hedge fund managers did," he said. Additionally, he shared that he had lost a large portion of his wealth because of his divorce. He gave his ex-wife more than half of their assets—not because he had to but because he didn't want to drag their kids through endless court battles. He said he felt like a pushover but added, "In a divorce, you need to have at least one adult in the room, and there was no one else to play that role, so it had to be me." He often complained about not making it in "the big league"—not becoming a billionaire—despite having more money than he or his children would ever need. They regularly took lavish ski trips with his girlfriend, and even his ex-wife and her new boyfriend joined from time to time.

Which pitfalls is the patient engaged in?

1. Overlooking his inner spark of talent.
2. Comparing and despairing.

3. Imagining a perfect alternate universe that makes you feel ungrateful and miserable in this one.

4. All of the above.

The correct answer is 4, all of the above. The patient is comparing and despairing. As we saw in chapter 11, it's not his fault—our brain evaluates rewards based on what we see around us. But simply knowing about the comparing neurocircuitry, along with being aware of these additional pitfalls, can help rein in the comparing brain.

Importantly, the patient mentioned going on ski trips with his new girlfriend, his children, and his ex-wife and her beau without realizing what an achievement that is, one that many people wouldn't be able to attain. Being wealthy and having a cordial divorce do not usually go hand in hand. Divorce can be brutal when there's wealth involved, because when there are a lot of assets, people often end up in drawn-out legal battles, fueled by expensive lawyers who know how to win but leave relationships in ruins. The fact that he was able to navigate this challenge and have his family come out of it relatively unscathed—remaining on good terms with his ex-wife—was a huge accomplishment. It speaks to his inner spark of talent: remarkable interpersonal acumen and incredible parental instincts.

The patient never recognized his amicable divorce as a worthy accomplishment because, in our culture, secure traits—amicability, preserving and promoting close relationships, and so on—are not considered valuable societal commodities. They will not earn you status symbols such as a fancy house, an impressive art piece, social recognition, or fine jewelry, so it was easy for him to brush it aside as irrelevant when measuring his talent and accomplishments.

AFTERWORD

# Your Secure Practice

Emotional learning is implicit—this means a lot of it takes place without our even realizing it. Think of falling in love. We can feel it happening, sometimes very quickly, sometimes more slowly, and if we look back, we can identify some crucial moments when things shifted. But the process itself—how we got from meeting a stranger to living with them and sharing a home—had many little points of inflection that occurred along the way, and we won't be able to identify each and every one.

Becoming secure takes a similar path. Following the principles laid out in this book, you will become more secure with time, but it will occur gradually and you won't be able to pinpoint exactly how, when, and where it happened. Instead, you have to keep at it—you have to develop a secure practice. And you can't do it alone.

A secure practice might mean making an effort to meet a trusted friend for lunch once a week, calling a secure parent regularly, or watching movies or reading books with secure themes. It also means minimizing

## AFTERWORD

insecure interactions so your emotional balance sheet tilts decisively toward security.

The good news is that maintaining a secure practice isn't hard; it's actually very rewarding. At its core, all it really asks is that you build a rich social life with CARRP people and fill your world with CARRP SIMIs. Why would anyone complain about surrounding themselves with a great group of people day in and day out? Yes, there's an initial adjustment period, but once you get through that, you'll be well on your way. And even when life throws the occasional insecure curveball, you'll have your secure village to help you through it.

This book was written to help you create your own secure practice. I've included many of the tools that I use in Secure Therapy and Secure Coaching so that you, too, can benefit from them. As with learning to play golf, pickleball, or any other sport, you won't always get it right the first time—or even the ninety-ninth time. But the process itself is part of the reward. And as long as you keep practicing, you will grow, you will learn, and you will thrive.

Now all that's left is to roll up your sleeves and begin.

# Acknowledgments

Writing this book has shaped both my thinking and my life. Along the way, I've been inspired by a constellation of people—colleagues, friends, family, mentors, and the patients who shared their experiences with me. Each played a role, whether through a conversation, quiet encouragement, shared laughter, or moments of reflection.

Some informed the science, others challenged my outlook. Some walked with me during the hard parts, others simply believed in the work. Your support, insight, and care live in these pages. Thank you for being part of this journey.

# Index

**A**
acceptance, 234
action potentials, 57–58
activating strategies, 105–7, 137, 151–52
ADHD, 65–67
adolescence, 178–79
agreeableness, 211–12
alcoholism, 180–81
alternative universe, imagining, 234–36, 239, 241, 245–47
amino acids, 125
animals
   birds, 26, 62, 67, 186, 188
   caregiving in, 244
   cats, 125
   collaboration in, 186
   comparisons made by, 185–86
   dogs, 125, 188
   mass calamities and, 124–25
   mice, 174–75, 179–80
   primates, 185–86, 188
   rats, 41–42, 47–48, 186, 188
anxiety dimension, 64, 72–74, 86–87, 89
anxious attachment style, ix, 5, 8, 73, 95–122, 158–59, 165, 213
   anxiety and avoidance dimensions in, 86
   brain energy and, 64
   burnt-out mode in, 112, 114
   "Call me, we need to talk" experiment and, 88
   CARRP and, 101, 102, 106–10, 112–15
      Appendix Rule and, 112–14
      CARRP versus non-CARRP behaviors, 109, 113
   Cyberball effect and, 161
   dopamine receptor gene and, 98–99
   and freeing your biology, 117–19
   gaslighting and, 101–5, 107, 110

# INDEX

anxious attachment style (*cont.*)
   materialism and, 163
   obstacles to becoming secure, 101–6
     gaslighting, 101–5, 107, 110
     protest-regret cycle, *see* protest-regret cycle
   orchids and dandelions analogy and, 98–99, 108, 233
   origin of, 97–101
     poor parenting hypothesis, 97–98
   perceptual abilities in, 95–102, 106, 108, 112, 114, 116, 119, 126, 158, 204, 228
   in Relationship Structures Questionnaire, 86
   and repositioning of relationships, 114
     Wall Tennis with Love tool for, 114–15, 157
   SIMIs and, 101, 102, 113–15
   upside of, 116–17
   workshop on, 120–22
*Aplysia*, 2–3
apologizing, 151–53, 165, 228
   Mea Culpa Rule, 227, 238
Appendix Rule, 112–14, 146, 147
arguments, 152, 228
artificial intelligence (AI), 225–26
assertiveness, 208–11, 240
ATP (adenosine triphosphate), 57, 58
*Attached* (Levine and Heller), 5
attachment gaslighting, 101–5, 107, 110
attachment homeostasis, 133–35

attachment styles, ix, 5, 48, 71–93
   beliefs and assumptions about, 169–70
   as biological talents, 204
     *see also* hidden sparks of talent
   brain energy and, 55–56, 64–65, 102
   "Call me, we need to talk" experiment and, 71, 87–88
   changes in, throughout life, 179
   in childhood and adulthood, 178
   closeness-distance paradox in, 128–29, 130
   dimensions in, 64, 72–74, 86–87, 89
   Relationship Structures, Questionnaire for, 8, 73–87
     attachment interpretation, 86–87
     attachment style average scores, 85
     attachment style with specific people, 74, 75, 79–81
     dimensions, 78–79, 81, 86–87
     general attachment style, 74, 75, 76–79
     plotting attachment topography, 82–83
     samples of, 83–84, 91–93
   research on, 73
   spectrum of, 92
   in teen years, 178–79
   testing your knowledge of, 155–66
     Amanda example, 156–57
     Cherry example, 158–59
     Luke example, 159–60
     Mercedes example, 160–61
     Micah example, 161–64
     Mirabel example, 164–66

workshop on, 88–93
   birthday party argument
      example, 88–91
   Relationship Structures
      Questionnaire example, 91–93
*see also* anxious attachment style;
   avoidant attachment style;
   fearful avoidant attachment
   style; secure attachment style
attention, 35
authority figures, 209
availability, 30–32, 46
   *see also* CARRP; protest behavior
avoidant attachment style, ix, 5, 8, 73, 123–42
   advantages of, 126, 204
   anxiety and avoidance dimensions in, 86–87
   brain energy and, 64
   "Call me, we need to talk" experiment and, 88
   CARRP and, 128–38
      CARRP versus non-CARRP behaviors, 135, 136, 139–42
      guided exercise, 139–42
   closeness and distance in, 126–29, 130, 135–38
   deactivating strategies in, 137, 139–40
   delegating work and, 159–60
   explaining need for space to others in, 138
   fearful avoidant attachment style versus, 153
   origins of, 126–28
   pitfalls in, 132–38
      closeness overdose, 135–38
      expecting others to go it alone, 132–33
      messing with attachment homeostasis, 133–35
   in Relationship Structures Questionnaire, 86–87
   SIMIs and, 124, 134, 137–38
   vicious cycle in, 135
   *see also* fearful avoidant attachment style
avoidance dimension, 64, 72–74, 86–87, 89

# B

behavioral activation, 176
biological diversity, 8, 203–4
biological needs and environmental fit, 232–33, 238, 239
birds, 26, 62, 67, 186, 188
bone marrow transplants, 203–4
boundary setting, 189–91, 227–28
brain, xiii–xiv, 13–14
   action potentials in, 57–58
   in adolescence, 178–79
   amount used, 56–57
   amygdala in, 60, 64
   collaboration and, 8, 187–89, 191–92
   comparison and, 183–87, 198, 237
   connectedness and, 29–30
   DNA in, 2–4, 41
   dopamine and, 98–99
   exclusion and, 16–17, 20, 22, 23
   functional MRI of, 16, 20, 60, 63, 96, 183–84

brain *(cont.)*
   glucocorticoid receptors in, 41
   hippocampus in, 41
   limbic system in, 188
   memories and, 2–3, 177, 222
   neurogenesis in, 42
   neurons in, 57–58, 60–62, 221–22
   neurotransmitters in, 58
   nucleus accumbens in, 60
   oxytocin in, 244
   prefrontal cortex in, 61
   relearning and, 221–22
   reshaping of, 3, 39–44, 48, 49, 179, 222
   reward areas of, 60, 64, 183–84, 244
   safety and, 20, 25–26, 29, 61–63, 72, 128
   secure attachment and, xv, 1–9
   secure spiel and, 212–13
   security of relationships and, 62–63
   SIMIs and, 47–48
   social support's effects on, 27–28, 39–44
   stillfacing and, 7, 17–19
brain energy, 8, 54, 55–69, 190, 193
   attachment styles and, 55–56, 64–65, 102
   blood flow and, 60
   boundaries and, 190
   crowdsourcing and, 61–62, 67–69, 72
   dimensions and, 72
   freeing up, 60–61
   glucose in, 58, 60, 63
   maximizing, 65–69
   crowdsourcing a task, 67–69
   Nathan example, 54–67
   supply and demand in, 59–61, 63, 69, 72
Brennan, Kelly, 73
Brigham Young University, 28
burnt-out mode, 112, 114

## C

Carnegie Mellon University, 28
CARRP (consistent, available, responsive, reliable, predictable), 8, 28–35, 49, 229, 232, 238, 250
   anxious attachment style and, 101, 102, 106–10, 112–15
   Appendix Rule and, 112–14
   CARRP versus non-CARRP behaviors, 109, 113
   availability in, 30–32, 46
   avoidant attachment style and, 128–38
   CARRP versus non-CARRP behaviors, 135, 136, 139–42
   guided exercise, 139–42
   boundaries and, 190, 191
   collaboration and, 190, 196
   consistency in, 30–32, 46
   fearful avoidant attachment style and, 145–47, 149
   interventions, 150–51
   interventions, 33, 46, 101, 110, 161, 190
   Appendix Rule in, 112–14, 146, 147

## INDEX

for fearful avoidants, 150–51
Marsha example, 113–14
predictability in, 31–32, 46
reliability in, 31–32, 46
responsiveness in, 30–32, 46
SIMIs and, 45–47, 101, 102, 115, 134, 137–38, 145–47, 250
in psychoanalysis example, 45–46
cats, 125
cattle, 124
causality, 170, 171–82
in attachment styles, 178
careful approach to, 175–76
separation anxiety example, 172–73, 176
workshop on, 180–82
*C. elegans*, 125
*Cell*, 2, 3
childhood experiences, 44
recounting of, 177
separation anxiety, 172–73, 176
*see also* causality
Clark, Catherine, 73
closeness
activating strategies, 105–7, 137, 151–52
avoidant attachment style and, 126–29, 130, 135–38
closeness-distance paradox, 128–29, 130
in fearful avoidant cycle, 144–46
overdose of, 125–38
safety risks of, 124–26
*see also* distance

Coan, Jim, 63
codependence, 227–28
cognitive behavioral therapy (CBT), 176
Cohen, Sheldon, 28
collaboration, 40, 110
assessing potential for, 186–87, 188
boundary setting and, 189–91
brain and, 8, 187–89, 191–92
CARRP and, 190, 196
effective, 191–93
ending, 192
workshop on, 193–201
Cindy example, 198–99
Collaborative Assessment Scale, 193–97, 228
Missy example, 197–98
Tamara example, 200–201
collective effervescence, 191–92
Columbia University, 26
comparison, 183–87, 193, 198, 236–38, 239, 246–47
computer smoke experiment, 96, 126
connectedness
brain and, 29–30
building a secure village, 32–35
hyperconnectedness, 23, 26–29, 49, 228, 237
benefits of, 27–28
SIMIs and, 47
*see also* CARRP
consistency, 30–32, 46
*see also* CARRP
consumerism, 163
control, perception of, 21–23, 47
cooperation, 211

*257*

# INDEX

crowdsourcing, 61–62, 67–69, 72
Cutuli, Debora, 41
Cyberball effect, 7, 15–23, 49, 157, 160–61
   experiments on, 15–17, 19, 20, 26
   stillfacing, 7, 17–19, 107

## D

dandelions and orchids analogy, 98–99, 108, 233
deactivating strategies, 29, 137, 139–40, 144–45, 151
decision making, 205–6, 208, 212
deer, 124, 185
delegating responsibility, 159–60
deliberation, 205–6, 208
distance
   avoidant attachment style and, 126, 127
   closeness-distance paradox, 128–29, 130
   deactivating strategies, 29, 137, 139–40, 144–45, 151
   in fearful avoidant cycle, 144–46
   social and solitary behavior, 125
   *see also* closeness
divorce, 246, 247
DNA, 2–4, 41, 203
dogs, 125, 188
dopamine, 98–99

## E

Earl, Slexis, 26
eating, 59
Ein-Dor, Tsachi, 96
electric shock experiments, 209

emotions, 21, 25, 53–54, 55, 60, 188, 198, 222, 249
   collaboration and, 189
   dopamine receptor gene and, 98
   energy and, 56–59, 64
   negative, 151–52, 206
   rules of secure engagement, 226–27, 228
      Mea Culpa, 227, 238
      Only One Person Is Allowed to Be Upset at a Time, 226–27, 238
energy, 56–59
   brain's use of, *see* brain energy
   emotional, 56–59
   tissue survival times and, 59
environmental enrichment, 8, 37, 39, 41, 43, 47–49, 65, 118
environmental fit, 232–33, 238, 239
Erasmus Medical Center, 27
evolution
   action potentials and, 57
   comparison and, 185–87
   exclusion and, 17
   molecular diversity and, 8, 203–4
   safety and, 61–62, 124–25, 157
   self-domestication in, 211–12
   social adaptiveness and, 179
   survival of the fittest in, 211
exclusion, 23
   brain and, 16–17, 20, 22, 23
   Cyberball effect, 7, 15–23, 49, 157, 160–61
   experiments on, 15–17, 19, 20, 26
   stillfacing, 7, 17–19, 107
   evolution and, 17

## INDEX

negative effects of, 20–23, 28
protection and survival and, 20, 25–26
exercise, 59
Experiences in Close Relationships questionnaire, *see* Relationship Structures Questionnaire
exposure treatments, 176

### F

fairness, 187–88, 199
Fayant, Marie-Pierre, 16
fearful avoidant attachment style, ix, 8, 72, 143–54, 161, 164–65, 176
  anxiety and avoidance dimensions in, 87
  arguments and, 152
  avoidant attachment style versus, 153
  and building a secure village, 146–49, 150
    steps in, 149
  "Call me, we need to talk" experiment and, 88
  CARRP and, 145–47, 149
    interventions, 150–51
  closeness-distance cycle in, 144–46
  moving to security from, 153–54
  negative emotions in, 151–52
  in Relationship Structures Questionnaire, 87
  SIMIs and, 145–48
  Stop Yourself in Your Tracks and Apologize, tool for, 151–53, 165
  *see also* avoidant attachment style

financial advisers, 208–10
Fliessbach, Klaus, 183
forgive and forget, 198
Fraley, R. Chris, 73, 74, 96
Freud, Sigmund, 46
Frisbee game, 15–16
Fyer, Abby, 2

### G

gaslighting, 101–5, 107, 110
genes
  dopamine receptor, 98–99
  of lab mice, 175
  neuropeptide receptor resemblance, 125
Gillath, Omri, 71, 87
Gonsalkorale, Karen, 16
Guan, Zhonghui, 2
Guinness World Records, 124

### H

happiness and well-being, xiii, 27, 28, 45, 69, 117–18, 192, 237–38
  Harvard study on, 237
Harari, Yuval Noah, 40
Harvard University, 17, 96, 117–18, 237
Hazan, Cindy, 73
health and disease, xiv, 27–28
  health-care providers, xiv, 186–87, 208–10
Hebb, Donald, 47–48
Heller, Rachel, 5
hidden sparks of talent, 8, 203–20, 240

# INDEX

hidden sparks of talent (*cont.*)
    impediment inventory and, 215–20
        constant input example, 216
        corporate worker example, 218
        stubborn wife example, 217
    not seeking out the best environment for maximizing, 233, 239
    overlooking or misinterpreting, 230–31, 238, 239, 240, 241, 245–47
    secure spiel and, 212–13
        creating, 213–15
    uncovering in Secure Therapy, 205–6
Holt-Lunstad, Julianne, 28
Hudson, Nathan, 48
Human Flourishing Program, 117–18
hyperconnectedness, 23, 26–29, 49, 228, 237
    benefits of, 27–28
    SIMIs and, 47
    *see also* CARRP

## I

Iceland, 27
indecisiveness, 205–6, 208
independence, 56, 86, 129, 151, 153, 216, 228
individuality, 126, 228
inner sparks of talent, *see* hidden sparks of talent
insecure attachment styles, 8
    brain energy and, 56, 64
    CARRP and, 34
    collaboration and, 186
    negative thoughts and emotions in, 206
    relationships and, 53–54
    *see also* anxious attachment style; avoidant attachment style; fearful avoidant attachment style
interpersonal therapy, 176

## J

job search, xiv–xv

## K

Kahneman, Daniel, 192
Kandel, Eric, 2–3

## L

learning, 3
    relearning, 221–22
Life & Brain center, Bonn, 183
"life is a mixed bag" paradigm, 234–36
lightning strikes, 124
lizards, 186
*Lucy*, 56

## M

MacDonald, Geoff, 126
materialism, 163
Mea Culpa Rule, 227, 238
meaning, 169
    in life, 21–23, 47, 118
memories, 2–3, 177, 222
mice, 174–75, 179–80
Mikulincer, Mario, 96
Milgram, Stanley, 209–10
molecular diversity, 8, 203–4

# INDEX

**N**
Nasiriavanaki, Zahra, 96
National Institutes of Health, 193
negative thoughts and emotions, 151–52, 206, 234–38, 239
nervous system, 3, 18, 29, 57, 97, 102, 104, 108, 112, 113, 128
neuroscience, 207
    epigenetics in, 3
    secure-focused, 6–7
    *see also* brain
New York University, 27
Nobel Prize, 40, 192
noise sensitivity, 232–33
NPR-1 (neuropeptide receptor 1) gene

**O**
obedience experiments, 209–10
Olympics, 40
Only One Person Is Allowed to Be Upset at a Time Rule, 226–27, 238
orchids and dandelions analogy, 98–99, 108, 233
oxytocin, 41–42

**P**
pain, social and physical, 22
parenting
    anxious attachment style and, 97–98
    avoidant attachment style and, 126–28
past, examining, 8, 44
    *see also* causality
people-pleasing the secure way, 227–30
phenylalanine, 125

predictability, 31–32, 46
    *see also* CARRP
primates, 185–86, 188
procrastination, 205–6, 208
protest behavior, 124, 129–33, 135, 144–45, 156
    in protest-regret cycle, 29, 105, 106–7, 118
protest-regret cycle, 101–2, 105–6, 115
    activating strategies in, 105–7
    additional non-CARRP incident in, 108
    attachment backlash in, 107, 113
    attachment system activation in, 106
    burning of social bridges in, 108–10
    burnt-out mode and, 112, 114
    creating a secure script to ride the protest-activation wave, 111
    flowchart of, 109, 113
    protest behavior in, 29, 105, 106–7, 118
    protest blowout in, 107
    reconciliation and residual resentment in, 107
    stages of, 106–8
psychoanalysis, 1–2, 6, 45–46
psychopathology, 207
psychotherapy, 176
    psychodynamic, 173, 207
    therapist-patient relationship in, 177–78
Purdue University, 15, 18

**R**
rats, 41–42, 47–48, 186, 188
Reichman University, 96

# INDEX

reindeer, 124
relationships, 44–45, 53–54
  attachment dimensions and, 73
  brain energy and, 64, 69
  ending, 156–57
  homeostasis in, 133–35
  insecure attachment patterns in, 53–54
  inventory of, 32–33
  physical tasks and, 63, 67–69
  repositioning of, 114
    Appendix Rule in, 112–14, 146, 147
    Wall Tennis with Love in, 114–15, 147, 157
  secure, 189
Relationship Structures Questionnaire, 8, 73–87
  attachment interpretation, 86–87
  attachment style average scores, 85
  attachment style with specific people, 74, 75, 79–81
  dimensions, 78–79, 81, 86–87
  general attachment style, 74, 75, 76–79
  plotting attachment topography, 82–83
  samples of, 83–84, 91–93
reliability, 31–32, 46
  *see also* CARRP
responsiveness, 30–32, 46
  *see also* CARRP
resting potential, 57

## S

safety, 20, 25–26, 29, 61–63, 72
  brain and, 20, 25–26, 29, 61–63, 72, 128
  evolution and, 61–62, 124–25, 157
  exploration and, 128–29
  risks of closeness, 124–26
Salinas, Joel, 27
*Sapiens* (Harari), 40
Sapienza University of Rome, 41
Schnall, Simone, 63
Schwartz, Jimmy, 2–4, 193
secure attachment style, ix, xii–xv, 5, 48, 53, 73, 204
  anxiety and avoidance dimensions in, 72, 86
  brain and, xv, 1–9
  brain's energy use and, 55–56, 64
  "Call me, we need to talk" experiment and, 71, 87, 88
  in Relationship Structures Questionnaire, 86
Secure Coaching, 8–9, 221–47, 250
  people-pleasing the secure way, 227–30
  pitfalls to secure stance, 230–39
    comparing and despairing, 236–38, 239, 246–47
    ignoring biological needs and environmental fit, 232–33, 238, 239
    imagining alternative universe, 234–36, 239, 241, 245–47
    not seeking out the best environment, 233, 239
    overlooking or misinterpreting

# INDEX

sparks of talent, 230–31, 238, 239, 245–47
self-defeating and insecure mental patterns, 234–38, 239
real-time interventions, 223–25
using AI for, 225–26
rules of secure engagement, 226–27, 228
   Mea Culpa, 227, 238
   Only One Person Is Allowed to Be Upset at a Time, 226–27, 238
workshop on, 240–47
   Dee Dee example, 242–44
   Loren example, 244–46
   not making it in the big league example, 246–47
   Sylvia example, 240–42
secure environment
   recalling memories in, 177
   SIMIs in, *see* SIMIs
   transformative effects of, 37–39, 42–44
secure interactions, xiii
   *see also* SIMIs
secure life, pillars of, *see* CARRP
secure practice, 249–50
secure priming, 208, 209, 222
Secure Priming Therapy (Secure Therapy), xiii–xiv, 6–9, 45, 114, 127, 147, 152, 165–66, 170, 203, 208, 212, 223, 225, 240, 250
   secure spiel in, 212–13, 242
      creating, 213–15
      Dee Dee example, 214

uncovering hidden sparks of talent in, 205–6
*see also* Secure Coaching
secure spiel
   brain and, 212–13
   creating, 213–15
secure village, building, 32–35, 146–49, 150
self-domestication, 211–12
self-worth and self-identity, 21–23, 47
separation anxiety, 172–73, 176
Shaver, Phillip, 73
shopping, xiv
SIMIs (seemingly insignificant minor interactions), 8, 43–45, 222, 238, 242
   anxious attachment style and, 101, 102, 113–15
   avoidant attachment style and, 124, 134, 137–38
   brain and, 47–48
   CARRP and, 45–47, 101, 102, 115, 134, 137–38, 145–47, 250
      in psychoanalysis example, 45–46
   creating, 49
   fearful avoidant attachment style and, 145–48
   hyperconnectedness and, 47
   opportunities for, 47
smallpox, 40
social adaptiveness, 179
social and solitary behavior, 125
social conventions, 209–10
social defeat paradigm, 175

# INDEX

social environment, changing, 42–43, 49
social interactions, day-to-day, *see* SIMIs
social media, xiv, 22, 163, 228–29, 236–38
social support
   brain and, 27–28, 39–44
   health benefits of, 27–28
   *see also* connectedness
Southern Methodist University, 48
sparks of talent, *see* hidden sparks of talent
starlings, 26
stillfacing, 7, 17–19, 107
   still face experiment, 17–18
Stopping Yourself in Your Tracks and Apologizing, 151–53, 165
stress hormones, 41
stroke, 60
subway experiment, 209–10
survival of the fittest, 211

## T
Tal, Orgad, 96
television, 236
theory of mind, 189
*Thinking, Fast and Slow* (Kahneman), 192

Tronick, Ed, 17
Tversky, Amos, 192

## U
Université de Paris, 16
University of California, Davis, 16
University of Illinois, 74, 96
University of Kansas, 71
University of Massachusetts, 17
University of Plymouth, 63
University of Toronto, 126
University of Virginia, 63

## V
valine, 125
van der Velpen, Isabelle, 27
VanderWeele, Tyler, 117
video game experiment, 183–84

## W
Waller, Niels, 73
Wall Tennis with Love tool, 114–15, 147, 157
Weil, Simone, 35
Wesselmann, Eric, 18
Williams, Kip, 15–16, 20
wolves, 186
World Health Organization, 40